READ IT AGAIN!
Pre-K Book 2

By Libby Miller and Liz Rothlein
Illustrated by Libby Miller

GoodYearBooks

An Imprint of ScottForesman
A Division of HarperCollinsPublishers

To Owen and Esther, my mom and dad, who
encouraged and believed in me. I thank you!
—L.M.

To my loving daughter, Kim, a dedicated
mother who meets the difficult challenges of a
modern-day woman with strength and dignity.
—L.R.

GoodYearBooks
are available for most basic curriculum subjects plus many
enrichment areas. For more GoodYearBooks, contact
your local bookseller or educational dealer. For a complete
catalog with information about other GoodYearBooks,
please write:

GoodYearBooks
Scott, Foresman and Company
1900 East Lake Avenue
Glenview, IL 60025

Cover illustration by Yoshi Miyake.
Design by Street Level Studio.
Copyright © 1994 Libby Miller and Liz Rothlein.
All Rights Reserved.
Printed in the United States of America.

ISBN 0-673-36042-3

1 2 3 4 5 6 7 8 9 10 - PC - 02 01 00 99 98 97 96 95 94 93

CONTENTS

Introduction

Selected Books and Activities

INTRODUCTION

Interest in using trade books in classrooms across the United States is increasing as many leading educators point to the importance of bringing children and the best in books together. Among them is Bernice Cullinan (1987), former president of the International Reading Association, who has spoken out on the power of trade books to overcome aliteracy, a term used for those who can read but don't or won't read. William Bennett (1986), former U.S. Secretary of Education, is another. He has recommended using more trade books in the elementary classroom as a way to overcome "the deadening quality of what children are given to read."

Evidence of the success of integrating trade books into the reading curriculum is clear. Research has repeatedly shown that there is no better way to teach children how to read than to read to them and with them (Doake, 1979; Durkin, 1966; Holdaway, 1979; International Reading Association, 1986a, 1986b; McGee & Richgels, 1990; Morrow & Smith, 1990; Schickedanz, 1983, 1986). In addition to learning to read through programs rich with literature, children develop personal reading preferences and special interests; they are motivated to read books of their own choice. This is of key importance, since proponents of literature-based programs agree that the success of a reading program should be measured in terms of the number of students who eventually establish the habit of reading for independent learning, personal pleasure, and continued growth (Sutherland & Arbuthnot, 1991).

There are additional compelling reasons. Reading to children helps increase their vocabularies. According to Elley (1989), young children can learn new vocabulary words as they listen to teachers reading carefully chosen picture books. This researcher found that when teachers explained unfamiliar words in the story, gains measured between pre- and post-reading vocabulary tests were about 40 percent.

Developing a love and appreciation for good literature should be a positive and enriching part of a young child's school experience. The words used to tell a good story can delight the senses and stimulate the imagination. And, through exposure to the best in picture books, young children can learn about others as they learn about themselves.

The attitudes children develop toward reading are of great importance. As Bruno Bettelheim (1981) insightfully stated, "A child's attitude toward reading is of such importance that, more often than not, it determines his scholastic fate. Moreover, his experience in learning to read may decide how he will feel about learning in general, and even about himself as a person." Ulrich Hardt (1983) has supported this view, saying, "Children will become readers only if their emotions have been engaged, their imaginations stirred and stretched by what they find on printed pages. One sure way to make this happen is through literature."

Therefore, it is important that teachers are trained in methods and techniques for integrating literature into the curriculum and are provided with the appropriate materials. Many publishers are responding to their needs by publishing guidebooks and kits. *Read It Again! Pre-K Book 2* is an example of these new resources. The eight units that follow provide educators with imaginative teaching ideas for use with easily accessible, quality books that children like.

Children in preschool through grade one will benefit from the materials in this book as they develop a love of reading and thinking. The activities emphasize the interactive processes of speaking, listening, reading, and writing. They involve children in music, art, process writing, cooking, geography, and poetry. The discussion questions suggested for each book reflect the taxonomy developed by B. S. Bloom and others (1956) and focus on developing higher-order thinking skills, requiring children to analyze, synthesize, and evaluate.

Read It Again! Pre-K Book 2 is easily adaptable to almost any classroom setting. The activities can be presented to either large or small groups. They are designed for different levels of ability and can be used to encourage independent work.

Read It Again! Pre-K Book 2 is also an excellent resource for parents. At-home activities are provided for each of the eight books presented. The suggested books and activities will help parents develop in their children an appreciation for literature and build skills these young learners need to become effective, involved readers.

Objectives

Read It Again! Pre-K Book 2 is designed to enable children to develop vital thinking and learning skills. By engaging in the activities proposed in the following eight units, children will make important first steps in reaching the following objectives developed by the National Council of Teachers of English (1983):

- Realize the importance of literature as a mirror of human experience, reflecting human motives, conflicts, and values.

- Be able to identify with fictional characters in human situations as a means of relating to others; gain insights from involvement with literature.

- Become aware of important writers representing diverse backgrounds and traditions in literature.

- Become familiar with masterpieces of literature, both past and present.

- Develop effective ways of talking and writing about varied forms of literature.

- Experience literature as a way to appreciate the rhythms and beauty of the language.

- Develop habits of reading that carry over into adult life.

Features

Read It Again! Pre-K Book 2 focuses on the following eight easy-to-find books, which have a proven track record of success with children:

Hattie and the Fox by Mem Fox
Mary Wore Her Red Dress and Henry Wore His Green Sneakers by Merle Peek
Oh, a-Hunting We Will Go by John Langstaff
The Napping House by Audrey Wood
The Secret Birthday Message by Eric Carle
Snow Magic by Harriett Ziefert
The Very Busy Spider by Eric Carle
The Blue Balloon by Mick Inkpen

Basic information is provided for each book: author, illustrator, publisher and publication date, number of pages, and a list of other works by the same author. This information is followed by a summary of the book and an introduction to use when presenting the book to children. Discussion questions, which foster higher-level thinking skills, follow. An oral language activity, designed to develop vocabulary and an understanding of a wide range of concepts, is also included.

The many suggestions for involving children in active learning which are presented in the Learning Center, Parent Bulletin, and Additional Activities sections make *Read It Again! Pre-K Book 2* particularly helpful to parents and teachers. These activities can easily be integrated into language arts, reading, and social science curricula.

• Each learning center section describes an activity designed to engage children's interest. A pictorial representation of the activity is included, which can be adhered to a piece of cardboard, stapled to a dowel rod or a stick, and then placed in a flowerpot. This marker can either be changed as each new center activity is introduced, or more than one flowerpot can be used at once in order to allow several centers to operate concurrently. A list of materials needed for use at each center is provided along with directions for completing the activity.

• The parent bulletin is designed to be duplicated and sent home with each child. It provides information about the book being used and describes activities parents can do at home that will reinforce what children are learning in school.

• A number of additional activities and ideas also are provided. (Reproducible worksheets needed for many are included.) Some activities are designed for a group; others are best suited for individual participation. Teachers and parents can determine which activities are most appropriate to meet each child's needs based on his/her abilities and interests.

The evaluation sheet provided for each book is another important feature. These worksheets help teachers gain information about what each child has learned from the activities provided.

Guidelines for Using This Book

Before using the activities in *Read It Again! Pre-K Book 2*, it is important that the teacher or parent present the selected books in interesting and meaningful ways. When children hear a story enthusiastically presented, their enjoyment is virtually assured. At the same time, the parent or teacher is modeling the very skills that children will need as they read on their own. When reading aloud, the following suggestions may be helpful:

1. Establish a regular schedule for reading aloud.
2. Practice reading the book in advance in order to acquaint yourself with the story.
3. Have a prereading session to set the stage for the book. Tell children about the title and author/illustrator of the book, provide an introduction or purpose for listening to the story, and introduce key vocabulary words.
4. Create a comfortable atmosphere with minimal distraction.
5. Read with feeling and expression. If the spoken dialogue is to sound like conversation, you need to pay careful attention to pitch and stress.
6. As often as possible, hold the book so that everyone can see the print as well as the illustrations.
7. Allow the children to participate in the story whenever possible. Occasionally, you may want to stop and ask the children what they think might happen next or how the story might end.
8. Provide opportunities to respond to the story. Although it is not necessary for children to respond to every story that is read, they can benefit from such follow-up activities as discussion questions, dramatizations, art activities, and so on.

The flexible format of *Read It Again! Pre-K Book 2* allows the teacher or parent to use this resource in a variety of ways. The amount of time allotted to each book will depend on several factors, including the children's ages and grade levels and the flexibility of timing and scheduling.

References

Bennett, William J. *First Lessons: A Report on Elementary Education in America.* Washington, DC: U.S. Government Printing Office, 1986.

Bettelheim, Bruno. "Attitudes Toward Reading." *Atlantic Monthly,* Nov. 1981, p. 25.

Bloom, B. S., M. B. Englehart, S. J. Fuerst, W. H. Hill, & D. R. Krathwohl. *Taxonomy of Educational Goals. Handbook I: Cognitive Domain.* New York: Longmans Green, 1956.

Cullinan, Bernice E. (ed.). *Children's Literature in the Reading Program.* Newark, DE: International Reading Association, 1987.

Doake, David. "Book Experience and Emergent Reading Behavior." Paper presented at Preconvention Institute No. 24, Research on Written Language Development, International Reading Association annual convention, Atlanta, April 1979.

Durkin, Dolores. *Children Who Read Early.* New York: Teachers' College Press, 1966.

Elley, W. B. "Vocabulary Acquisition from Listening to Stories." *Reading Research Quarterly,* 1989, vol. 24, pp. 174–187.

Hardt, Ulrich. *Teaching Reading with the Other Language Arts.* Newark, DE: International Reading Association, 1983, p. 108.

Holdaway, Don. *The Foundations of Literacy.* Toronto: Ashton Scholastic, 1979.

International Reading Association. "IRA Position Statement on Reading and Writing in Early Childhood." *The Reading Teacher*, Oct. 1986a, vol. 39, pp. 822–824.

International Reading Association. "Literacy Development and Pre-First Grade: A Joint Statement of Concerns About Present Practices in Pre-First Grade Reading Instruction and Recommendation for Improvement." *Young Children,* Nov. 1986b, vol. 41, pp. 10–13.

McGee, L. E., & D. J. Richgels. *Literacy Beginnings: Supporting Young Readers and Writers.* Boston: Allyn & Bacon, 1990.

Morrow, L. M., & J. K. Smith. *Assessment for Instruction in Early Literacy.* Englewood Cliffs, NJ: Prentice-Hall, 1990.

National Council of Teachers of English. "Essentials of English." *Language Arts,* Feb. 1983, vol. 60, pp. 244–248.

Schickedanz, J. *Helping Children Learn About Reading.* Washington, DC: National Association for the Education of Young Children, 1983.

Schickedanz, J. *More Than the ABCs: The Early Stages of Reading and Writing.* Washington, DC: National Association for the Education of Young Children, 1986.

Sutherland, Z., & M. H. Arbuthnot. *Children and Books* (8th ed.). Glenview, IL: ScottForesman, 1991.

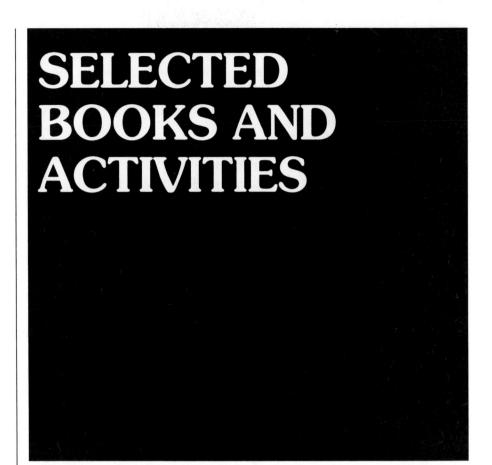

SELECTED BOOKS AND ACTIVITIES

HATTIE AND THE FOX

Author
Mem Fox

Illustrator
Patricia Mullins

Publisher
Bradbury Press, 1986

Pages
30

Other Books by Fox
*Shoes from Grandpa;
Wilfrid Gordan McDonald
Partridge; Possum Magic;
Guess What?; Koala Lou;
Night Noises; With Love, at
Christmas*

Summary
Hattie the hen lives in a farmyard with a horse, cow, pig, sheep, and goose. She senses that there is danger in the bushes but the other animals pay little notice until a fox reveals himself completely. Young children will enjoy the story as the cumulative tale builds to the final surprise.

Introduction
Do not read the title of the book. Instead, read the first page about Hattie seeing a nose in the bushes. Then ask the children to predict what they think might be in the bushes. Write their predictions on the chalkboard. After reading, look together at the predictions. Did anyone come close to guessing who had been hiding?

Discussion Questions

1 What would you do if you were Hattie and saw a nose in the bush? Why? (Answers may vary.)

2 Why was the fox hiding in the bushes? (Answers may vary.)

3 Why were the animals afraid of the fox? (Answers may vary.)

4 Which of the animals should be the most afraid of the fox? Explain. (Answers may vary.)

5 What do you think would have happened if the cow hadn't frightened the fox away? (Answers may vary.)

6 What did you like most about the story? (Answers may vary.) Is there anything you didn't like? (Answers may vary.)

7 If you could write a new ending to this story, what would you write? Why? (Answers may vary.)

ORAL LANGUAGE ACTIVITY

Activity
Sing and dramatize the following barnyard song using the tune of "The Wheels on the Bus."

Materials: 6" x 6" pieces of construction paper, 3" x 24" pieces of construction paper (or sentence strips), crayons or markers, and a stapler.

Directions
1. Together, make a list of the kinds of animals found on a farm. Write the children's responses on the chalkboard. Next, have the children decide on the color of each farm animal and the sound it makes.

The	animal color	animal	on the farm	says	animal sound
The		hen	on the farm	says	cluck, cluck
The		goose	on the farm	says	honk, honk
The		pig	on the farm	says	oink, oink
The		horse	on the farm	says	neigh, neigh
The		cow	on the farm	says	moo, moo

2. Use the completed list to sing the new song to the tune of *The Wheels on the Bus.*

> The red hen on the farm says, "Cluck, cluck, cluck, cluck, cluck, cluck, cluck, cluck, cluck."
> The red hen on the farm says, "Cluck, cluck, cluck," all day long.

3. Give each child a 6" x 6" square of construction paper on which to illustrate and label a barnyard animal (Figure A). Staple the completed picture to a 3" x 24" piece of paper or sentence strip (Figure B) to fit around the child's head.

A.

B.

LEARNING CENTER ACTIVITY

Directions

Use the animals on pages 4 through 6 to create flannelboard characters that may be used by the children in the retelling of *Hattie and the Fox*. Color the animals, laminate, and cut out. Adhere small strips of flannel or fine sandpaper to the backs of the animals. (If you have a magnetic chalkboard, tape magnetic strips to the backs of the animals for storytelling.) Place a tape recorder at the learning center so that children, either individually or in groups, can tell their own versions of *Hattie and the Fox*.

From *Read It Again! Pre-K Book 2*, published by GoodYearBooks. Copyright © 1994 Libby Miller and Liz Rothlein.

STORYBOARD ANIMALS

From *Read It Again! Pre-K Book 2*, published by GoodYearBooks. Copyright © 1994 Libby Miller and Liz Rothlein.

HATTIE AND THE FOX

PARENT BULLETIN/HOMEWORK

Name _____ Date _____

This week we are reading *Hattie and the Fox* by Mem Fox. It is a story about some farm animals (a sheep, cow, horse, goose, pig, and hen) that were frightened by a fox in the bushes. Help your child learn more about farm animals through the following activities:

Monday: Fold a piece of 8 1/2" x 11" paper into fourths. Write the names of the following farm animals in each box: sheep, cow, hen. In the fourth box, write *My Farm Animal Book*. Have your child draw the animals above the animal names. This page will become the cover of the book.

Tuesday: Ask your child to choose one of the three animals from Monday's activity. Write the name of the animal at the top of an 8 1/2" x 11" page and then have your child draw a picture of the animal below the name. Ask your child to think of how the animal helps human beings. (For example, gives them milk to drink, wool to make clothes, etc.) Write what is dictated to you on a sheet of paper. Then help your child develop a sentence(s) using the words and ideas they have dictated. (For example, Cows give us milk to drink.) Write the sentence(s) under the illustration of the animal.

Wednesday, Thursday: Read the sentence(s) that was developed on Tuesday. Then follow the same procedure used on Tuesday, with your child selecting one of the animal words, creating an illustration of that animal, dictating words about that illustration, and finally writing a sentence about the animal. Staple the completed pages together and re-read.

Friday: Have your child bring the book to school to share with classmates.

Parent's Signature_____

From *Read It Again! Pre-K Book 2*, published by GoodYearBooks. Copyright © 1994 Libby Miller and Liz Rothlein.

Name _____ Date _____

1. This section evaluates the child's ability to hear the initial sound of "f" as in fox. Say the following pairs of words and have the child respond by raising a hand when the pairs of words begin with the sound of "f." Circle "yes" if the child responds correctly or "no" if the child responds incorrectly. Give the following example before beginning the evaluation:

Practice

fox - foot   Tell the child to raise his/her hand because the two words begin with the same sound of "f."

fox - apple   Tell the child not to raise his/her hand because the two words do not begin with the sound of "f."

A.	fox - fire	yes	no	E.	fox - face	yes	no
B.	fox - fat	yes	no	F.	fox - box	yes	no
C.	fox - socks	yes	no	G.	fox - finger	yes	no
D.	fox - farm	yes	no	H.	fox - rocks	yes	no

2. This activity evaluates the child's concepts of print.

Directions (for worksheet on page 10)

Duplicate the worksheet on page 10 and distribute it. Have each child cut apart the words at the top of the page on the solid lines and paste them, in order, in the long narrow box under his/her name. Then, ask everyone to illustrate the sentence in the large box using crayons.

A. Did the child paste the words in order from left to right? Yes ___ No ___
B. Are all of the words "right-side-up"? Yes ___ No ___
C. Does the child's picture relate to the sentence? Yes ___ No ___
D. Did the child place the period at the end of the sentence? Yes ___ No ___

Ask each child to read the words and point to each word as he/she reads it.

E. Is the child able to "read" the sentence? Yes ___ No ___
(Remember, reading at this level probably means that the child memorized the sentence.)
F. Does the child match the spoken word to the written word while reading and pointing? Yes ___ No___

Name _____ Date _____

fox	Hattie	sees	.	a

From *Read It Again! Pre-K Book 2,* published by GoodYearBooks. Copyright © 1994 Libby Miller and Liz Rothlein.

HATTIE AND THE FOX

Additional Activities

1 Farm Animal Bulletin Board

Materials: Butcher paper, paint, speech bubble.

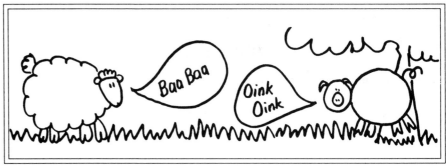

Activity

A. Talk together with the children about the kinds of animals found on a farm. Make a sketch of each animal on the chalkboard, and write the words for the sound it makes next to the sketch.

B. Ask children to make their own pictures of barnyard animals. Help them make a speech bubble and print the words that tell what their animals say inside.

C. Children should cut out their animals and speech bubbles and add them to a farmyard mural.

2 Clay Animals

Provide clay for the children and encourage them to make the animals that are in the story.

3 The Baby Farm Animal Book

Make two columns on the chalkboard or on a large sheet of paper. Label the top of one side **Animal Names** and label the other side **Baby Animal Names.** List the animals that are characters in the story. Then discuss with the children that babies of animals are often called something else. For example, a baby horse is called a colt. Make a corresponding list of baby animal names under the column **Baby Animal Names.**

Animal Names	Baby Animal Names
horse	colt
cow	calf
hen	chick
goose	gosling
pig	piglet
sheep	lamb

Additional farm animals and their babies may be added to the list. On the chalkboard write: **A baby _____ is called a _____.** Using the list above, have the children fill in the blanks with the appropriate animal and animal baby names. The activity sheet on page 15 may be used to make a class book.

4 Tongue Depressor Puppets

Materials: 6" x 6" pieces of construction paper, tongue depressors.

Activity
Place children in cooperative pairs. Have each child in a pair choose three animals from the story that he/she wishes to illustrate. Tell everyone to draw their animals as big as the paper, outline the animals with black crayon, color them, and then cut them out. Staple the animals to the tongue depressors.

When complete, re-read the story. As you read, ask children to hold up the correct animal and join in the response. For example, each time the goose appears, those who have drawn a goose should hold up their pictures and say together, "Good grief!"

5 Field Trip

Plan a field trip to a farm or petting zoo where the children can see and perhaps touch some of the animals that are in *Hattie and the Fox*. After the trip is over, write a class experience story on large chart paper. Have the children draw pictures of the experiences. Cut the pictures out and place around the story.

Use the story to have children:
    A. Locate key words
    B. Find words that begin with certain letters
    C. Find like words
    D. Find compound words

6 Animal Graph

Materials: Box of animal crackers, math graph on page 16, 5 oz. paper cups.

Activity
Place a handful of animal cookies in paper cups (one cup per child).

1. Duplicate the graph on page 16 and give each child a copy. Have children draw a picture of each of the animals (found in the box of cookies) in the boxes at the bottom of the graph.

2. Place a handful of animal cookies in paper cups and give each child one cup.

From *Read It Again! Pre-K Book 2*, published by GoodYearBooks. Copyright © 1994 Libby Miller and Liz Rothlein.

HATTIE AND THE FOX

3. Have the children estimate how many cookies they think are in their cups. Ask them to write their anwers in the box with one star.
4. Have children take out their cookies, one at a time, and place them on their graph.
5. Ask the following questions:
   A. Which animal do you have the most of?
   B. Which animal do you have the least of?
   C. Do you have any sets that are the same or equal?
6. Have children count the number of cookies found in the cup and write the number in the box with two stars.

7 Tissue Paper Animals

Materials: Assorted tissue paper colors, heavy stock paper (10" x 10"), white glue, brush, black felt-tipped permanent marker.

Reread the story of *Hattie and the Fox.* Have children pay particular attention to the artwork. Ask them to tell you how they think the artist made the pictures. Then explain that the illustrations in this book are collages. These collages are made with torn paper. Explain what a collage is and demonstrate how it is made using the steps below:

Activity
1. Have children choose one of the animals in the story of *Hattie and the Fox.*
2. Tear tissue paper into small pieces (Figure 1).
3. Water down the white glue (equal amounts of white glue and water).
4. Using a paintbrush, have children brush the white glue on the heavy stock paper (Figure 2).
5. Place the torn paper on the glue, overlapping the pieces and covering the paper (Figure 3).
6. Brush an additional coat of the glue mixture over the tissue paper.
7. Let dry.
8. Use a black marker to make an outline of the animal that was chosen (Figure 4). Cut the animal out.
9. Draw a scene from *Hattie and the Fox* (Figure 5).
10. Glue the animal to the front of the scenery (Figure 6).

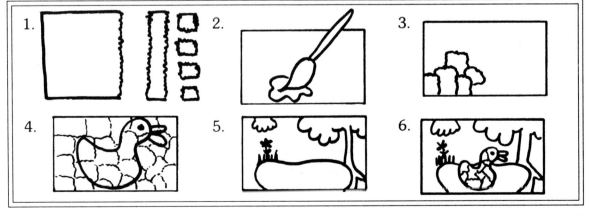

8 "What Next?"

A. Re-read *Hattie and the Fox*.

B. Discuss surprising situations that children could encounter in the classroom. Write children's suggestions in the form of sentences: I can see a _____ in the room; I can see a _____ on the teacher's desk; I can see a _____ on the wall; I can see a _____ out the window.

C. Have children choose words or phrases, different from those in the story, that could be used when they make the discovery: "Oh my!," "Oh no!," "My, my!," "Goodness gracious!," "Gee whiz!," etc.

D. Write one of the new situations on the board following the model in the box below, and reread.

I can see a *mouse* in the room.

"Oh my!" said _____ . (child's name in blank)

"Goodness gracious!" said _____. (child's name in blank)

"Gee whiz!" said _____. (child's name in blank)

"What next?" said _____. (child's name in blank)

E. Write each line of the new story on individual pages and have children illustrate the sentences. Put together into a book.

9 Word Book

Write the following sentence on the chalkboard: Hattie sees the f_____. Then cluster words like "fox" that begin with the sound of "f" (foot, feet, fire, fish, fairy, finger, fishermen, fan, farm, face, fig, flower, etc.)

Use the activity sheet on page 17. Have the children choose a word to use in the blank and illustrate the sentence in the box. (Be sure that Hattie is in the picture with the "f" word.) Put children's individual pages together to make a class book.

From *Read It Again! Pre-K Book 2*, published by GoodYearBooks. Copyright © 1994 Libby Miller and Liz Rothlein.

A baby _____

is called a _____ .

ANIMAL CRACKER GRAPH

* I think there are _____ cookies in the cup.

** I counted _____ cookies in the cup.

6					
5					
4					
3					
2					
1					

From *Read It Again! Pre-K Book 2*, published by GoodYearBooks. Copyright © 1994 Libby Miller and Liz Rothlein.

Hattie sees the f _____ .

MARY WORE HER RED DRESS AND HENRY WORE HIS GREEN SNEAKERS

Adaptor
Merle Peek

Illustrator
Merle Peek

Publisher
Ticknor & Fields, 1985

Pages
20

Other Books by Fox
The Balancing Act; Roll Over; A Counting Song

Summary

Mary Wore Her Red Dress and Henry Wore His Green Sneakers is a picture book version of a folk song from Texas. Merle Peek's illustrations highlight different animals and the type and color of clothing they are wearing as they go to a birthday party.

Introduction

Ask children if they have any clothing that is red (green). Next, ask what their favorite colors are. Then show them the cover of the book *Mary Wore Her Red Dress and Henry Wore His Green Sneakers*. Tell them to be on the lookout for their favorite colors as you read the story.

Discussion Questions

1 Ask the children to name the animals found in the story. Are the animals like real animals? (No, they wear clothes; Katy lives in a house.)

2 Where are the animals going? (They are going to a birthday party.)

3 Do you think the story is a real story or a pretend story? (Answers may vary.) Explain.

4 What other kinds of forest animals do you think might like to go to Katy's party? What do you think they might wear? (Answers may vary.)

5 What kind of hat is Katy wearing? (birthday hat) Why do you think Katy wore it all day long? (Answers may vary.)

6 How old is Katy? (She is 8 years old.) Where can you find out? (We can count the candles on her cake, which is pictured on the cover.)

7 What kinds of presents do you think Katy's friends gave her? (Answers may vary.) If you were going to Katy's party, what would you give her as a gift? (Answers may vary.)

ORAL LANGUAGE ACTIVITY

Mary Wore a White Baker's Hat and Henry Wore a Red Beanie

Hats can be a useful tool in generating interesting and stimulating vocabulary-building activities. There are many different kinds of hats: fire hats, police hats, bakers' hats, sailor hats, bonnets, fezes, beanies, caps, berets, straw hats, three-cornered hats, Red Cross hats, nurse hats, etc.

Send a note home requesting that children bring a hat to school. Collect enough hats so that each child has one. Begin the activity by asking the children to tell about their hat using words that describe color, style, and usage.

Have children put on their hats while singing the following song to the tune of "Mary Had a Little Lamb."

<u>Mary</u> wore <u>a white baker's hat</u>, <u>white baker's hat</u>, <u>white baker's hat</u>.
<u>Mary</u> wore <u>a white baker's hat</u>, all day long.

Add verses so that each child has a chance to sing about his/her hat. As the hats are being shared, replace Mary's name with another child's. Change the underlined words to words describing the new hat.

_____ wore _____, _____, _____.
_____ wore _____, all day long.

LEARNING CENTER ACTIVITY

Pin the Clothes on the Line

This activity is designed not only to develop patterning skills using clothing pattern cards, but also to increase small motor dexterity by hanging the cards on a clothesline using clothespins.

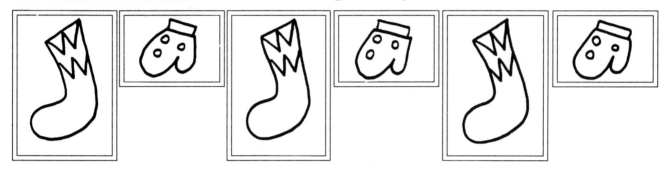

Materials: Clothesline, clothespins, picture cards, pattern cards.

Directions

1. Place a copy of page 21, the Activity Center Marker, at the learning center. Duplicate the pattern cards on pages 22–25. In addition, duplicate 10 sets of sock and mitten cards on pages 26 and 27.

2. Cut out and laminate the pattern cards and the sock and mitten cards.

3. Hang a clothesline, clothespins, and sock and mitten cards in a place where children can easily reach them.

4. Use the pattern cards on pages 22–25 for the following activities:

   A. Children can place a pattern card in front of them, sort the sock and mitten cards, and hang the cards on the clothesline to make a duplicate pattern and/or continue the pattern.

   B. Show children a pattern card for a few seconds, then turn it over, and ask them to repeat the pattern from memory.

   C. Children can use the sock and mitten cards to lay out a pattern and then challenge another child to duplicate it.

From *Read It Again! Pre-K Book 2*, published by GoodYearBooks. Copyright © 1994 Libby Miller and Liz Rothlein.

LEARNING CENTER ACTIVITY MARKER

MARY WORE HER RED DRESS AND HENRY WORE HIS GREEN SNEAKERS

Pin the Socks and Mittens on the Line

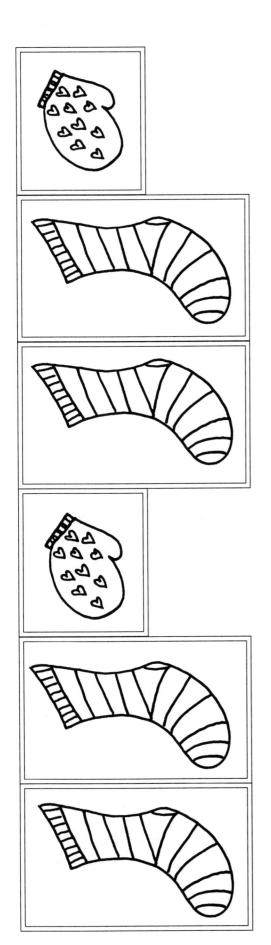
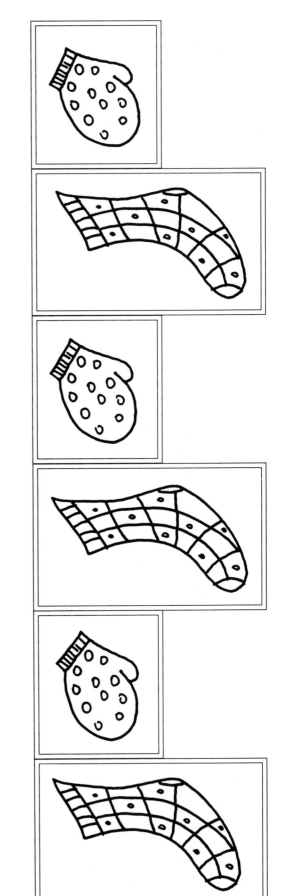

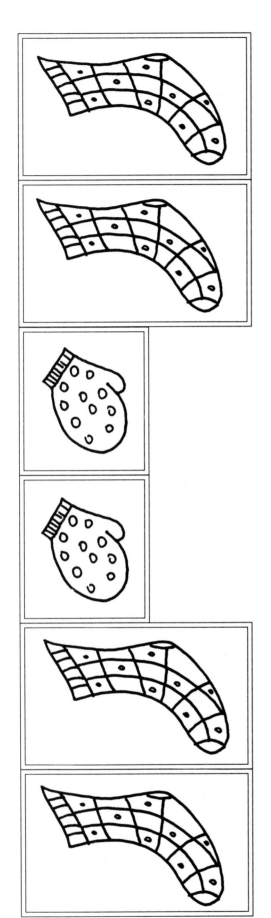
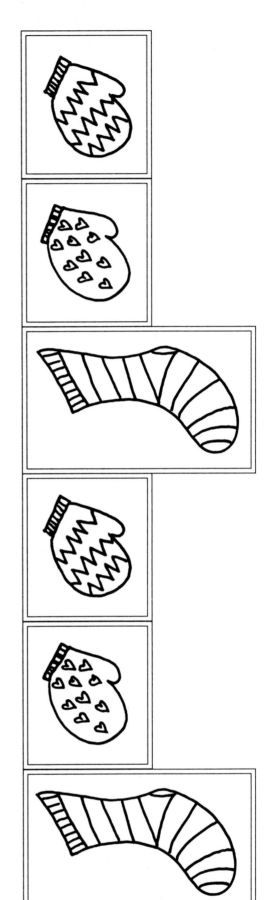

24 READ IT AGAIN!
PRE-K BOOK 2

From *Read It Again! Pre-K Book 2*, published by GoodYearBooks. Copyright © 1994 Libby Miller and Liz Rothlein.

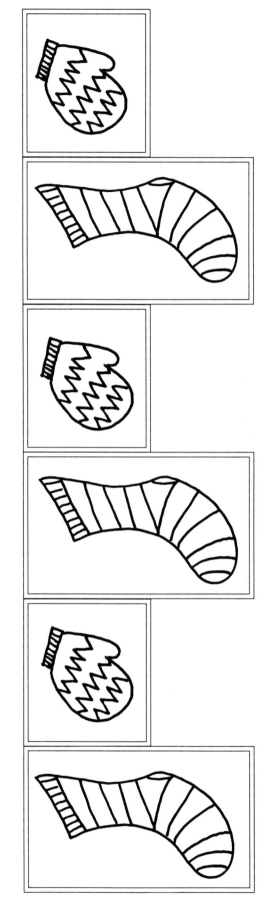

MARY WORE HER RED DRESS AND HENRY WORE HIS GREEN SNEAKERS

PARENT BULLETIN/HOMEWORK

Name _____ Date _____

We will be reading *Mary Wore Her Red Dress and Henry Wore His Green Sneakers* by Merle Peek in school this week. The book is a repetitive folk song from Texas. The illustrations depict animals on their way to a birthday party wearing clothing of various colors and styles. Throughout the week, help your child carry out the following directions:

Monday: Read for 10 minutes wearing your favorite colors. Draw a picture showing how you looked. Bring your picture to school on Tuesday.

Tuesday: Read for 10 minutes wearing two different socks (socks that don't match). Draw a picture showing how you looked. Bring your picture to school with you on Wednesday.

Wednesday: Read for 10 minutes wearing your favorite hat. Draw a picture showing how you looked. Bring your picture to school with you on Thursday.

Thursday: Read for 10 minutes wearing your mommy's or your daddy's shoes. Draw a picture showing how you looked. Bring your picture to school with you on Friday.

Parent's Signature_____

MARY WORE HER RED DRESS AND HENRY WORE HIS GREEN SNEAKERS

EVALUATION

Name_____ Date_____

1. Give the child a copy of the book *Mary Wore Her Red Dress and Henry Wore His Green Sneakers.*

   A. Ask the child to show you the front of the book.
   Is the child able to identify the front of the book?   Yes_____ No_____
   B. Ask the child to show you the back of the book.
   Is the child able to identify the back of the book?   Yes_____ No_____

2. Open the book to the first page.

   A. Ask the child to point to a letter.
   Does the child understand the concept of a letter?   Yes_____ No_____
   B. Ask the child to point to a word.
   Does the child understand the concept of a word?   Yes_____ No_____

3. Ask the child to open the book to the first page of *Mary Wore Her Red Dress and Henry Wore His Green Sneakers.* Have the child "read" from the text. Continue until he/she reaches "Katy wore her yellow sweater."

   A. Is the child able to "read" (recite) the passages?   Yes_____ No_____
   B. Is the child able to match the spoken word to the written word when pointing?   Yes_____ No_____

4. Point to the word "dress." Is the child able to find another word that looks just like it?   Yes_____ No_____

5. Begin a pattern using the sock and mitten cards from pages 26 and 27. Have the child continue the pattern using the picture cards. Is the child able to complete the pattern?   Yes_____ No_____

MARY WORE
HER RED
DRESS AND
HENRY WORE
HIS GREEN
SNEAKERS

Additional Activities

1 Class Dictionary of Clothing and Things to Wear

Write the letters of the alphabet down the left side of a long sheet of butcher paper. Have the children brainstorm types of clothing and things that can be worn. Write the name of each item next to the letter of the alphabet that it begins with. Children may draw pictures or cut pictures from magazines to illustrate each of the words.

Class Dictionary of Clothing and Things to Wear

A - apron, ascot, armor, anklets
B - boots, blouse, bow, beanie, bandanna (or bandana),
    belt, breeches, bonnet, beret, bow tie
C - coat, cap, cape, costume, crown
D - dress, dungarees
E - earmuffs, evening gown
F - fur coat, fez
G - gloves, galoshes, glasses, goggles, grass skirt, gown
H - hat, hood, helmet, headdress, headband, habit
I - ice skates
J - jeans, jacket, jumper, jerkin
K - kilt, kerchief, knickers, knapsack, kimono, knee socks
L - leggings, leotard
M - mittens, muff, mask
N - necklace, negligee, neckerchief, necktie
O - overalls, oxfords, obi
P - pants, poncho, pajamas, p.j.s
Q -
R - raincoat, rubbers, roller skates, robe
S - shirt, skirt, sombrero, socks, shorts, stockings, scarf,
    snowsuit, slippers, suspenders, shoes, snowshoes,
    shaw, sari, slacks, sweatshirt, sneakers
T - tie, turban, tunic, tiara, tutu, trousers, turtleneck
U - underwear
V - vest, veil
W - wet suit, wristwatch, wig, wristband
X -
Y -
Z - zoot suit

From *Read It Again! Pre-K Book 2*, published by GoodYearBooks. Copyright © 1994 Libby Miller and Liz Rothlein.

MARY WORE HER RED DRESS AND HENRY WORE HIS GREEN SNEAKERS

2 Our Shoe Book

Discuss why and when we wear shoes. In one column, make a list of the types of shoes that people wear (high heels, flippers, sneakers, thongs, cowboy boots, slippers, loafers, tennis shoes, sandals, hi-tops, galoshes, rubbers, flip-flops, dress shoes, patent leather shoes, ballet, etc.). In another column, write when they might be worn.

You may wish to make an overhead transparency of your own chart using the model below or you may wish to use the chart on page 32 to fill in the information. Use the completed chart as a reference for helping children make individual pages for a class book. (See page 33 for the frame for individual pages.)

Make a large shoe for the cover of the book. Place the children's pictures from page 33 inside the shoe.

1. Child's Name	2.	3. his/her	4. Kind of Shoe Color and Style	5. When Shoe Is Worn
Maria	wore	her	cowboy boots	when *riding on a horse*
Brian	wore	his	red galoshes	when *walking in the rain*
	wore			when
	wore			when
	wore			when

Brian wore his red galoshes, red galoshes, red galoshes.
Brian wore his red galoshes when walking in the rain.

The story may be sung to the tune of "Mary Had a Little Lamb."

Child's Name		his/her	Kind of Shoe Color and Style	When Shoe Is Worn
	wore			when
	wore			when
	wore			when
	wore			when
	wore			when
	wore			when
	wore			when
	wore			when
	wore			when
	wore			when
	wore			when
	wore			when
	wore			when
	wore			when

_____ wore _____ , _____

_____ wore _____ when _____ .

MARY WORE HER RED DRESS AND HENRY WORE HIS GREEN SNEAKERS

3 Green Cheese and Crackers

Make a snack of cream cheese and crackers. Divide the cream cheese into four individual small bowls. Tint the cheese by dropping a different color of food coloring into each bowl (red, yellow, green, blue). Allow the children to stir the cheese and then spread on crackers. Different shades of each color can be made by adding additional food colors. As a follow-up, obtain sample color cards from a paint store for different shades of red, yellow, blue, and green paint. Cut these apart and put in envelopes (one for each child). Allow time for the children to put them in order from lighter to darker shades.

4 My Favorite Color Is . . . .

Make a class color graph by writing "My Favorite Color Is _____" at the top of a large sheet of paper that has been divided into 3" x 3" squares (see page 35). Give each child a piece of 3"x 3" paper. Have each child write his or her name on the square. Then have each child bring the square to the graph and place it above his or her favorite color. Use as a math lesson for such concepts as more, less, and same.

My Favorite Color Is . . . .

		Bill					
		Liz		Kym			
Mary		Henry		Jorge			Ashley
red	blue	green	orange	black	brown	yellow	purple

5 Take a Color Walk

Divide the children into pairs. Give each pair a copy of page 36 which has 4 large squares. Assign every pair a color and give each a marker of that color. Then take a walk around the school. Ask children to take turns drawing a picture on their papers that represents something they have discovered that is the same color as their markers. After the walk is complete, allow time for the children to share their pictures.

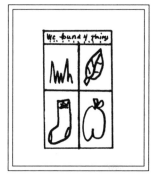

From *Read It Again! Pre-K Book 2*, published by GoodYearBooks. Copyright © 1994 Libby Miller and Liz Rothlein.

My Favorite Color Is . . . .

red	blue	orange	yellow	purple	black	brown	green

Names: _____ and _____ Date: _____

We found 4 _____ things
on our color walk at school.

6 "Can You Find the Color Red?"

Look for colors while singing the following to the tune of "Have You Seen the Muffin Man":

Oh, can you find the color red,
The color red, the color red.
Oh, can you find the color red,
On someone else's clothing?

Oh, yes I found the color red,
The color red, the color red.
Oh, yes I found the color red,
On (Child's name) (Name of piece of clothing)

7 Presto, Change-o

Bring in at least four white carnations, four bottles of water, and a food coloring set (red, green, yellow, blue). Put several drops of food coloring in each bottle of water. Put the carnations in the colored water. Have the children predict what they think will happen. Then have them observe what changes take place. Write an experience story describing what happened.

8 I Spy

Choose one child to be "IT." Have the child look around the room for a single object of a specific color. The child then whispers what the object is to the teacher.

"IT" then says, "I spy with my little eyes, something (color word). Three children are chosen to guess what the object is. If one of the children guesses correctly, he/she then becomes "IT." If the object is not guessed, "IT" has another turn.

9 When I'm Blue . . . .

Discuss that different colors may make people feel differently. Hold up color cards and ask the children to tell you how each color makes them feel.

10 Color Feast

Have a "Color Feast" by asking children to bring in foods for a specific color: red—apples, radishes, strawberries; yellow—cheese, lemons, bananas; green—lettuce, limes, beans, cucumbers, celery; orange—oranges, carrots; blue—blueberries. Classify the foods according to color. Have a taste treat by slicing and dicing so that everyone gets a taste of the foods of many colors.

From *Read It Again! Pre-K Book 2*, published by GoodYearBooks. Copyright © 1994 Libby Miller and Liz Rothlein.

MARY WORE
HER RED
DRESS AND
HENRY WORE
HIS GREEN
SNEAKERS

11 Color Blobs

Provide children with large sheets (12" x 18") of white or manila paper. Ask them to fold the paper in half. Then unfold the paper and drop a spoonful of red paint in the middle. Tell the children to refold the paper and press it flat. Next, reopen the paper to see the design. Repeat the process, adding other colors such as blue and yellow so the children can observe the process of color mixing.

Note: Color mixing also can be demonstrated by preparing three jars or bottles half-filled with water—one jar tinted with red food coloring, one with yellow, and one with blue. Then add some yellow water to the red water and discuss what happens. Next, add blue water to the red water and discuss what happens.

12 Related Books

Read other picture books emphasizing colors such as: *Is It Red? Is It Yellow? Is It Blue?* by Tana Hoban (Greenwillow, 1978); *I Dance in My Red Pajamas* by Edith Hurd (HarperCollins, 1982); *Color Zoo* by Lois Ehlert (HarperCollins, 1989); *John Burningham's Colors* by John Burningham (Crown, 1986); *Finding Red, Finding Yellow* by Betsy Imershein (Harcourt Brace Jovanovich, 1989); and *Colors* by Jan Pienkowski (Simon & Schuster, 1989). Discuss how these books are similar and how they are different.

13 Ice Cube Painting

Fill an ice-cube tray with water. Add a different color of food coloring (red, blue, green, and yellow) to each space. Place one craft stick into each space so that it touches the bottom and rests against the side. Then freeze until very hard (approximately 4 hours). Remove the colored ice cubes from the tray and place in a shallow dish. Give each child a large sheet of white paper. Seat everyone around the ice cubes so they can be easily reached. Show the children how to hold the

sticks and glide the ice cubes across the paper. Encourage the children to use all four colors of ice cubes so they will see the colors that are created when they are mixed.

OH, A-HUNTING WE WILL GO

Author
John Langstaff

Illustrator
Nancy Winslow Parker

Publisher
D. C. Heath & Co, 1986

Pages
32

Other Books by Langstaff
Frog Went A-Courtin'; Over in the Meadow; What a Morning! The Christmas Story in Black Spirituals; Climbing Jacob's Ladder: Heroes of the Bible in African-American Spirituals

Summary
Oh, a-Hunting We Will Go is a rhyming tale, often sung, about hunters and the creatures they seek. Each verse features a different animal, but the ending is always the same—the hunters let all the animals go.

Introduction
Read the title of the book *Oh, a-Hunting We Will Go* and show children the cover of the book. Then have a discussion to find out what children know about hunters: Do they know anyone who goes hunting? What kinds of things or creatures do people usually hunt for? Finally, ask children to predict the things they think the hunters in this book might find when they go hunting. List their predictions on the chalkboard or on a large sheet of paper. Later, after children are familiar with the story, compare these predictions with what they have actually heard (Additional Activity 1, page 50).

Discussion Questions

1 Which of the "creatures" that were caught would you most like to catch? Explain. (Answers may vary.)

2 Why do you think the hunters let all the creatures go? (Answers may vary.)

3 Were these good hunters? Why or why not? (Answers may vary.)

4 Do you think this story could really happen? Why or why not? (Answers may vary.)

5 What did the hunters take along on their hunting trip? (Answers may vary but might include: a net, plunger, horn, binoculars, rope.)

6 Do you think real hunters might use any of these things? Which ones? (Answers may vary.)

ORAL LANGUAGE ACTIVITY

Read and/or sing *Oh, a-Hunting We Will Go* with the children. Review the kinds of animals that were "hunted" in the story. Brainstorm and list additional animals that might be hunted. Write the names of the animals on the board or on a large sheet of paper. Next to the animals' names write a rhyming word indicating where the captured animal might be placed (there may be animals on the list that do not have a matching rhyming word).

Addition animals: snail—pail, jail; eel—banana peel; duck—truck; moose, goose—caboose; starfish—dish; shark—park; sheep—jeep; chipmunk—bunk, trunk; peacock—clock; rat, cat, bat—hat, vat; mice—ice; frog, hog—log; ants—pants; hen—pen; bug—jug, rug

On the chalkboard, write the verse shown below. Fill in the blanks with the animals and rhyming word selections that the children made during the brainstorming session.

Oh, a-hunting we will go,

A-hunting we will go;

We'll catch a _____

And put it in a _____

And then we'll let it go!

Make a class book using the cloze activity on page 41. Have children fill in the blanks using the cluster on the board. Cut the box out and paste it to the bottom of a 12" x 18" piece of drawing paper. Ask each child to illustrate his/her own verse in the space above the box.

From *Read It Again! Pre-K Book 2*, published by GoodYearBooks. Copyright © 1994 Libby Miller and Liz Rothlein.

Oh, a-hunting we will go,

A-hunting we will go;

We'll catch a _____

And put it in a _____

And then we'll let it go!

LEARNING CENTER ACTIVITY

Directions

Place the "Rhyming Hunt" activity marker (p. 43) at the center. Duplicate pages 44 through 47. Ask the children to color the pictures. Once the pictures are colored, laminate and cut apart. Mix the pictures together and place in an envelope or storage box at the learning center. Instruct children that they are to play Concentration by matching the pictures of the animals with what the hunters put them in (such as matching fox with box).

Play Concentration using the cards by following these directions:

1. Turn cards facedown.

2. Player 1 turns over two cards. If the cards match, the player may keep the cards. If the cards do not match, they are placed face down on the playing surface.

3. Then, Player 2 turns over two cards and follows the same procedures as Player 1.

4. Continue until all matches have been made.

From *Read It Again! Pre-K Book 2*, published by GoodYearBooks. Copyright © 1994 Libby Miller and Liz Rothlein.

A-HUNTING WE WILL GO

A-Hunting We Will Go

A-Hunting We Will Go

A-Hunting We Will Go

A-Hunting We Will Go

A-Hunting We Will Go

snake

A-Hunting We Will Go

A-Hunting We Will Go

A-Hunting We Will Go

A-Hunting We Will Go

cake

A-Hunting We Will Go

Concentration

fox

box

lamb

pram

goat

boat

bear

underwear

whale

pail

snake

cake

mouse

house

pig

wig

skunk

bunk

From *Read It Again! Pre-K Book 2*, published by GoodYearBooks. Copyright © 1994 Libby Miller and Liz Rothlein.

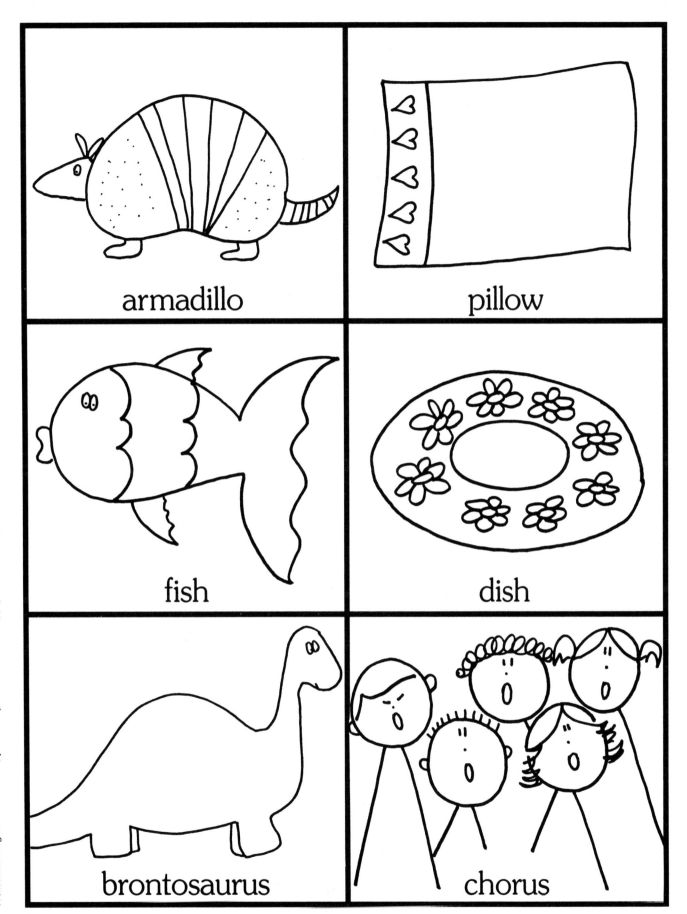

armadillo

pillow

fish

dish

brontosaurus

chorus

PARENT BULLETIN/HOMEWORK

Name _____ Date _____

We are reading a rhyming tale, *Oh, a-Hunting We Will Go* by John Langstaff and illustrated by Nancy Winslow Parker. This book is about four hunters who seek out various creatures but in the end always let them go. This book is written in rhyme and the verses can be sung to the music provided in the book. Please follow the directions below to help your child better understand the sound of the letter "H" as in "hunting":

Monday: Make a Hunter's Bag to keep "H" objects in. Make a large letter "H" on the outside of a brown paper bag and decorate. Add a handle using a strip of paper or a length of yarn.

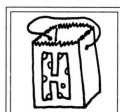

Tuesday: Ask your child to "go hunting" for objects and pictures of objects that begin with the letter "H." As he/she is hunting, chant "Oh, a-hunting we will go." Collect all of the "H" items and then, as your child names each item, place the items in the paper bag.

Wednesday: With a pencil, write the names of the "H" objects found during the "H" hunt on index cards or other small pieces of paper. Have your child trace over the words with crayons or markers.

hat

Thursday: Take the "H" pictures and objects out of the bag. Have your child match the "H" words to the objects.

Friday: Remind your child to bring his/her bag full of "H" words to school.

H words: hat, hair, hippo, hose, handkerchief, hanky, hi-tops, horse, heart, house, harp, hand, hanger, hog, hermit crab, heron, horn, helmet, helicopter, hatchet, hawk, hammerhead, hedgehog, hieroglyphic, hutch, hive, holly, honey, hoop, horsefly, hornet, hotel, horseshoe crab, horseshoe, hot, hummingbird, hyena

---

Parent's Signature _____

Name _____ Date _____

1. Give the child a copy of *Oh, a-Hunting We Will Go*.

    a. Ask the child to show you the front of the book.
    b. Ask the child to show you the back of the book.

	Yes	No
a. Is the child able to identify the front of the book?		
b. Is the child able to identify the back of the book?		

2. Open to the first page.

    a. Ask the child to point to a <u>letter</u>.
    b. Ask the child to point to a <u>word</u>.

	Yes	No
a. Does the child understand the concept of a letter?		
b. Does the child understand the concept of a word?		

3. Ask the child to open the book to the page with a picture of the four hunters. Have the child "read" from the text. Continue until he/she reaches the page with the goat on it.

	Yes	No
a. Is the child able to "read" (recite) the words?		
b. Is the child able to match the spoken word to the written word by pointing?		

4. Point to the word "hunting." Is the child able to find another word that looks just like it? Yes____ No____

OH, A-HUNTING WE WILL GO

Additional Activities

1 What Did the Hunters Catch . . . . And Then Let Go?

Have the children make a list of all the creatures that the hunters were looking for in the story: a fox, a lamb, a goat, a bear, a whale, a snake, a mouse, a pig, a skunk, an armadillo, a fish, a brontosaurus. Compare this list with the predictions that were made prior to reading the story.

2 A-Hunting We Will Go Rhyming Book

Materials: Pages 52 and 53, crayons and/or markers, pencils.

After reading, *Oh, a-Hunting We Will Go,* have children name the rhyming words. Write and illustrate the words on the board.

Place children in cooperative pairs. Have one child complete the page that says "The hunter found a _____," and have the second child in the pair complete the page that says, and put it in a _____."
After the pictures have been illustrated and the words written in the blanks, collect the pages and place them in a rhyming book.

The hunter found a ___,

and put it in a ___.

3 Oh, a-Hunting We Will Go Class Book

On index cards, write the names of the characters in the book and the places where the hunters put them. Fold the cards and put them in a "hat" (box, envelope, etc.). Have each child choose a word from the hat and illustrate his/her word on a blank sheet of paper. Children may refer to the Class Rhyming Book for the picture that represents the word. If there are more children than animals, more than one picture can be made for any given character.

Re-read the story and, as you do, ask children to come forward and hold up their illustrations for all to see at the appropriate time. Finally, staple the pictures together in the correct order, write the words from the text below the picture, put a cover on it, and you have a class book (or books) of *Oh, a-Hunting We Will Go.*

4 Keep on Hunting

In the story, the hunters always put the creatures in places that rhyme with the creatures' names. Write each creature's name on the chalkboard and then, as a group, think of other places for the creature that would still rhyme: a snake in a lake, a snake on a rake, a bear on a chair, a bear in the hair, a bear in the air.

From *Read It Again! Pre-K Book 2,* published by GoodYearBooks. Copyright © 1994 Libby Miller and Liz Rothlein.

5 The Hunters See "H" Words Phonics Classics Book

Materials: worksheet on page 54, crayons or magic markers, pencils.

Make a class sound book for the letter "H" by having the children cluster all the words they can think of that begin with the sound of "H" as in *hunting.* Write the words on the chalkboard so that the children can refer to them as they work. Additional "H" words include: house, hand, hat, hop, happy, head, helicopter, heel, helmet, hare, hair, high, hill, hole, hip, hog, hoe, honeydew, horn, horse, hospital.

Give each child a copy of page 52. Have everyone select and illustrate one of the "H" words on his/her page of the class book. Help children fill in the blank with the word that corresponds to the picture that each has drawn. Collect the completed pictures and put them together to make a book.

6 Hunter's Brew

The hunters were probably tired and thirsty when they finished their hunting trip. Help the children prepare some "Hunter's Brew" by following this recipe:

    3/4 cup lemonade-flavored drink mix
    1/2 cup strawberry-flavored drink mix
    2 quarts cold water
    1 quart ginger ale
    2 trays of ice cubes

Stir all the ingredients together. This recipe provides 1/2 cup servings for 30 children.

The hunter found a _____ ,

and put it in a _____.

The hunter sees a _____.

THE NAPPING HOUSE

Author
Audrey Wood

Illustrator
Don Wood

Publisher
Harcourt Brace Jovanovich, 1984

Pages
29

Other Books by Wood
Balloonia; Detective Valentine; Elbert's Bad Word; Heckedy Peg; King Bidgood's in the Bathtub; Quick as a Cricket; Three Sisters; Tugford Wanted to Be Bad; The Horrible Holidays; Little Penguin's Tale; Magic Shoelaces; Moonflute; Oh, My Baby Bear; Orlando's Littlewhile Friends; Presto Change-o; The Princess and the Dragon; Scaredy Cats; Tooth Fairy; Twenty-four Robbers

Summary
This is a cumulative tale in which a wakeful flea gets on top of a number of sleeping creatures (a snoring granny, a dreaming child, a dozing dog, a snoozing cat, and a slumbering mouse) and causes a commotion, with just one bite.

Introduction
Show children the cover of the book, and read the title. Then ask them to predict what they think the book will be about. What do they think a napping house is and what it would be like?

Discussion Questions

1 Do you think this story could really happen? Why or why not? (Answers may vary.)

2 If you were the snoring granny, how do you think you'd feel about having the child and all the creatures in bed with you? Explain. (Answers may vary.)

3 Why do you think they all decided to sleep on top of one another instead of finding their own space in which to sleep? (Answers may vary.)

4 Were the characters in this book unhappy because they were awakened and the bed broke? Explain. (Answers may vary.)

5 Describe the napping house. Would you like to live there? Why or why not? (Answers may vary.)

6 Which character do you think broke the bed? Why? (Answers may vary.)

ORAL LANGUAGE ACTIVITY

Activity
Sing and dramatize the napping house song (p. 57) using the tune of "The Farmer in the Dell."

Materials: Six chairs to represent the bed, six pieces of 6" x 6" construction paper, six 3" x 24" pieces of construction paper (or sentence strips), crayons or markers, and a stapler. (A sheet may be used for the dramatization.)

Directions
1. Place 6 chairs close together at the front of the room to represent the bed.

2. Give each child a sentence strip headband on which to place an illustration of a character from the book.

3. Give each child a 6" x 6" square of construction paper on which to illustrate and label a character from the story (granny, child, dog, cat, mouse, flea) (Figure A). Staple the completed picture to a 3" x 24" piece of paper (or sentence strip) (Figure B) to fit around the child's head.

A

B

4. Prior to singing the song, have children place themselves in the order in which they appear in the story (granny, child, dog, cat, mouse, flea). As the children sing the song, the child wearing the headband of the character currently being sung about takes his/her place in the appropriate chair.

After the sixth verse, the child with the flea headband should pretend to bite the mouse and get out of bed. The mouse will then pretend to scare the cat and get out of bed. The children continue singing until all of the characters are out of bed.

From *Read It Again! Pre-K Book 2*, published by GoodYearBooks. Copyright © 1994 Libby Miller and Liz Rothlein.

The granny's in the bed, the granny's in the bed,
Hi! Ho! the napping house, the granny's in the bed.

The child gets in the bed, the child gets in the bed,
Hi! Ho! the napping house, the child gets in the bed.

The dog gets in the bed, the dog gets in the bed,
Hi! Ho! the napping house, the dog gets in the bed.

The cat gets in the bed, the cat gets in the bed,
Hi! Ho! the napping house, the cat gets in the bed.

The mouse gets in the bed, the mouse gets in the bed,
Hi! Ho! the napping house, the mouse gets in the bed.

The flea gets in the bed, the flea gets in the bed,
Hi! Ho! the napping house, the flea gets in the bed.

The flea bites the mouse, the flea bites the mouse,
Hi! Ho! the napping house, the flea bites the mouse.

The mouse scares the cat, the mouse scares the cat,
Hi! Ho! the napping house, the mouse scares the cat.

The cat claws the dog, the cat claws the dog,
Hi! Ho! the napping house, the cat claws the dog.

The dog thumps the child, the dog thumps the child,
Hi! Ho! the napping house, the dog thumps the child.

The child bumps the granny, the child bumps the granny,
Hi! Ho! the napping house, the child bumps the granny.

The granny hops out of bed, the granny hops out of bed,
Hi! Ho! the napping house, the granny hops out of bed.

Everyone laughs and laughs, everyone laughs and laughs,
Hi! Ho! the napping house, everyone laughs and laughs.

Directions

1. Place the Napping House Learning Center Activity Marker (page 59) at the Learning Center.
2. Make 2 copies of the character cards on page 60.
3. Cut out the cards and glue them to index cards to make them into playing cards.
4. Laminate the cards.
5. Then play Concentration using the directions in the box below.

How to Play:

1. Turn all cards facedown.
2. Player 1 turns over two cards. If the cards match, the player may keep the cards. If the cards do not match, the player turns the cards facedown again on the playing area.
3. Player 2 then turns over two cards and follows the same procedures as Player 1 did.
4. Continue until all matches have been made.

From *Read It Again! Pre-K Book 2*, published by GoodYearBooks. Copyright © 1994 Libby Miller and Liz Rothlein.

THE NAPPING HOUSE

The Napping House	The Napping House	The Napping House	The Napping House
The Napping House	granny	The Napping House	The Napping House
The Napping House	The Napping House	granny	The Napping House

Concentration

granny

child

dog

cat

mouse

flea

THE NAPPING HOUSE

PARENT BULLETIN/HOMEWORK

Name _____ Date _____

We are reading *The Napping House* by Audrey and Don Wood. It is a story in which a wakeful flea gets on top of a number of sleeping creatures (a snoring granny, a dreaming child, a dozing dog, a snoozing cat, and a slumbering mouse), and causes a commotion with just one bite.

As we read *The Napping House,* we are reinforcing the order in which the characters appear in the story (sequencing), developing the concept of ordering by size, and building an understanding of spatial relationships (over, under, in, on, etc.).

To complete this week's homework, your child will need crayons, an 8 1/2" x 11" piece of paper, and a stapler.

Monday: Make an envelope in which to store the napping house characters. Fold an 8 1/2" x 11" piece of paper in half and staple along the edges (Figure A). On the front side of the envelope write *The Napping House* (Figure B) and on the back side have your child draw a picture of a house (Figure C).

Tuesday: Have your child draw pictures to illustrate the characters in the story. Characters should be drawn in accordance to their size in the story, the flea being the smallest and the granny being the largest. Cut out the pictures. Use the envelope for storage.

THE NAPPING HOUSE

Wednesday: 1. Have your child place the pictures in order from the smallest to the largest. Have your child point to the smallest, the largest. 2. Mix the characters up and have your child place them in order from the largest to the smallest.

Thursday: Using the pictures, have your child do the following:
1. Place the dog before the cat.
2. Place the cat after the child.
3. Place the granny over the mouse.
4. Place the flea below the dog.
5. Place the child in front of the cat.
6. Place the mouse behind the granny.
7. Continue in the same manner using the words: over, under, behind, below, in front of, between, on, above, next to, etc.

Friday: Please have your child return the envelope and pictures to school.

Parent's Signature _____

From *Read It Again! Pre-K Book 2*, published by GoodYearBooks. Copyright © 1994 Libby Miller and Liz Rothlein.

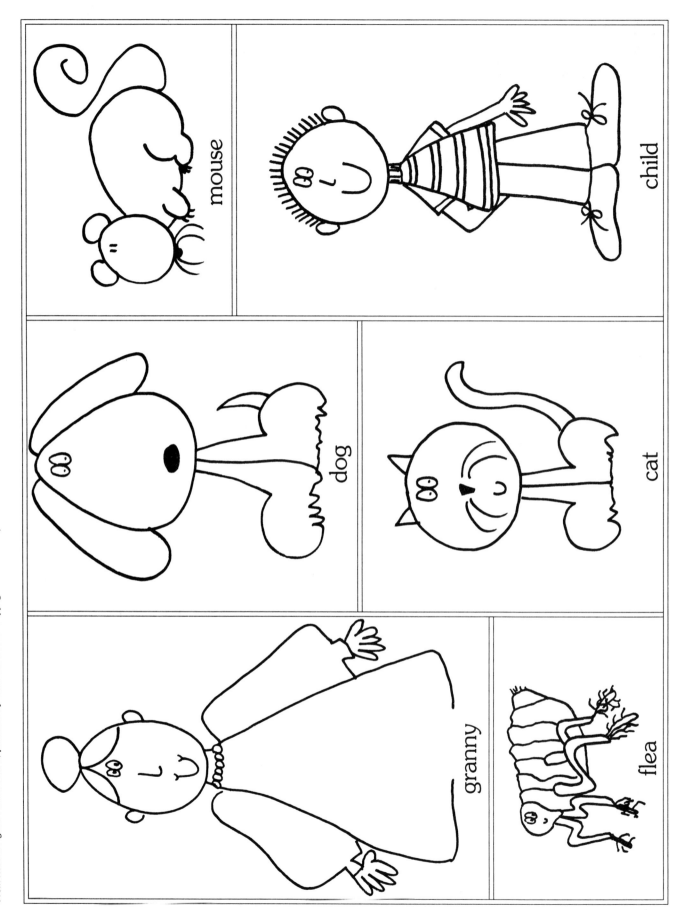

mouse

child

dog

cat

granny

flea

Use the character cards from page 63 to assess the following concepts: the ability of the child to order pictures by size, to demonstrate an understanding of spatial relationships; to sequence the characters in order of their appearance in the story of *The Napping House*.

1.   Have the child place the pictures from page 63 in order from the smallest to the largest.

Is the child able to order the pictures from the smallest to the largest?
yes __ no __

flea	mouse	cat	dog	child	granny

2.   Collect the pictures and place them in random order in front of the child. Have the child find the picture of the granny and place it directly in front of him/her on the table (or the floor). Ask the child to listen to the following directions and to use the pictures.

		YES	NO
A.	Put the dog above the granny.		
B.	Put the flea below the granny.		
C.	Put the cat in front of the flea.		
D.	Put the child behind the dog.		

3.   Collect the pictures and hand them to the child. Ask the child to place the pictures in the order that they got into the bed in the story. Yes _____ No _____

granny	child	dog	cat	mouse	flea

From *Read It Again! Pre-K Book 2*, published by GoodYearBooks. Copyright © 1994 Libby Miller and Liz Rothlein.

THE NAPPING HOUSE

Additional Activities

1 All Kinds of Houses

Materials: 12" x 18" manila or construction paper, crayons or markers.

Directions
After reading *The Napping House,* ask children to think of other kinds of houses (such as *The Eating House, The Exercising House*, and *The Reading House*). Write their suggestions on the chalkboard. Have each child select one of the houses from the list to illustrate.

Give each child a piece of paper and have him/her fold it in half (Figure A). Have the child draw a picture of the house he/she has selected on the front and write the name of the house across the top (Figure B). On the inside, ask the child to illustrate what happens inside the house (a child reading in a Reading House, a man exercising in the Exercising House, etc.) (Figure C). Finally, allow time for the children to share their illustrations and tell about their houses.

2 Describing Time

Obtain a big book copy of *The Napping House* or copy the text onto chart paper. Then cover the following describing words (adjectives) by taping strips of white paper (or use Post-It® tape) over them: cozy, snoring, dreaming, dozing, snoozing, slumbering. Next, re-read the story asking the children to provide different words that describe what is happening. Write these new words on the strips of paper and re-read the entire story, substituting the new words.

3 When I Take a Nap, I Dream About . . . .

After reading *The Napping House,* ask children what they thought each of the characters in the story dreamed about. Ask the children what they dream about when they sleep. Give children a copy of the worksheet on page 66 and have them draw a picture of themselves napping on the pillow. Ask them to draw a picture of their naptime dream in the dream bubble. Allow time to share pictures and/or put pictures together for a class book.

When I take a nap I dream about _____.

THE NAPPING HOUSE

4 Animals Live in Houses, Too

Materials: Page 68, a 5" x 6" piece of manila paper, either a 1" x 3" piece of construction paper or a short length of yarn, crayons, stapler.

Directions

Begin this activity with a brainstorming session, making a list of the many different kinds of animals that the children can think of. Draw and label their ideas on the blackboard or on a large sheet of paper. Next, have the children name the kind of "house" that the animal lives in. Draw and label the house pictures next to the animal pictures. (Examples: bird in a nest, a whale in the ocean, a pig in a sty, etc.)

Animals	Houses
whale 🐋 worm 🐛 bird 🐦	ocean 〰️ apple 🍎 nest

Place children in cooperative pairs to complete the activity. First, have the pairs decide on the animal and the animal's home that they wish to illustrate. Next, fold page 68 on the dotted line and staple along the edges to make a pocket envelope. On the outside of the envelope above the words, "A _____ lives in __ _____," have one child draw a picture of the animal's house (Figure A). Have the other child draw a picture of the animal on the 5"x 6" piece of paper (Figure B). Attach a yarn loop to the top of the paper or use the short strip of construction paper to make a pull tab. Slide the picture into the envelope. Complete the sentence by writing the appropriate words in the space provided.

A   B

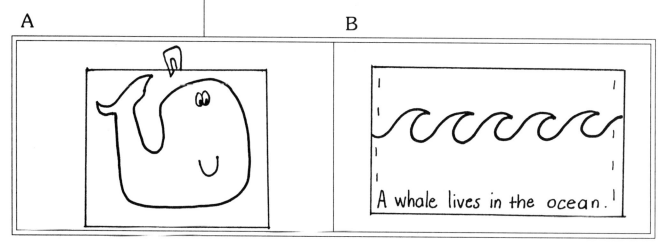

A whale lives in the ocean.

A _____ lives in _____ _____.

· ·

THE NAPPING HOUSE

5 To Nap or Not to Nap

Read other books about napping/sleeping such as *Goodnight Moon* by Margaret Wise Brown (HarperCollins, 1947); *Ira Sleeps Over* by Bernard Weber (Houghton Mifflin, 1972); *There's an Alligator Under My Bed* by Mercer Mayer (Dial Books for Young Readers, 1987); or *Bedtime for Frances* by Russell Hoban (HarperCollins, 1960). Then have a sharing time in which the children discuss reasons why they like to take a nap and reasons why they don't like to take a nap. Make a list of their reasons on a chart to use for further discussion.

Why I like to take a nap.	Why I don't like to take a nap.

6 Have You Seen the Napping House?
Sing the following song to the tune of "Do You Know the Muffin Man?"

Can you find the snoring granny, the snoring granny, the snoring granny?
Can you find the snoring granny, who sleeps in the cozy bed?

Can you find the dreaming child, the dreaming child, the dreaming child?
Can you find the dreaming child, who naps on the snoring granny?

Can you find the dozing dog, the dozing dog, the dozing dog?
Can you find the dozing dog, who naps on the dreaming child?

Can you find the snoozing cat, the snoozing cat, the snoozing cat?
Can you find the snoozing cat, who naps on the dozing dog?

Can you find the slumbering mouse, the slumbering mouse, the slumbering mouse?
Can you find the slumbering mouse, who naps on the snoozing cat?

Can you find the wakeful flea, the wakeful flea, the wakeful flea?
Can you find the wakeful flea, who bites the slumbering mouse?

Oh, yes I can, I found those things, I found those things, I found those things.
Oh, yes I can, I found those things, all sleeping in the napping house.

Before singing the song, make a simple outline of a house on a large piece of posterboard. Color and cut out the characters on page 63. Laminate or cover the characters with Contact® paper. On the back of characters, place the loop part of adhesive-backed Velcro®. Arrange the pictures in the house and then place the fuzzy part of the Velcro® on the house.

As the children sing the song, have them add the pictures in sequence to correspond to the words of the song.

7 A House of My Own
Provide a wide assortment of magazines and catalogs along with the following: 12" x 18" sheets of manila paper, scraps of construction paper, paste, markers, pastel chalk, wet sponge, crayons, and a copy of the book *The Napping House,* opened to the page where *all* the characters are piled on top of each other (just before the flea bites the mouse). Clip this page open and put on a shelf or hang on the wall (be sure it is visible, yet covered with plastic and/or out of reach of glue, markers, etc.). Tell the children to create their own illustration for this page, using different characters than those found in the book. Provide a place to hang the illustrations when they are completed. Note: These illustrations may be used later to write stories.

From *Read It Again! Pre-K Book 2,* published by GoodYearBooks. Copyright © 1994 Libby Miller and Liz Rothlein.

THE NAPPING HOUSE

8 Phonics: What Is in the Napping House?

Materials: one piece of 10" x 18" manila paper, one piece of 10" x 14" manila paper.

Activity
Gather the children on the floor. Cluster words that begin with the sound of "n" as in nap. Example: newt, nap, night, nightgown, napkin, nest, nose, nice, niece, nurse, nut, note, news, nine, etc. Be sure to write the word and illustrate its meaning so that the children will have a reference when they work on their cloze activity.

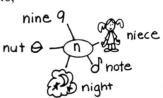

Write on the board in manuscript:

A _____ is in the napping house.

Have children take turns filling in the blank with one of the words from the "n" cluster. Fill in the blank and point to the words as they are being read. Then have each child choose one of the words from the "n" cluster to fill in the blank for his/her individual napping houses.

To make the napping house:

1. Fold the first sheet of 12" x 18" paper in half.

2. Staple along sides and bottom.

3. Add windows, door, a flower box, etc.

4. Measure 6" from the top of the second sheet of 12" x 18" paper and fold down.

5. Cut 1" away from the sides of the 12" x 18" piece of paper.

6. Illustrate an "n" word in the space provided.

7. Fold down the top of the paper for the roof. Write: A _____ is in the napping house.

8. Slide "n" picture into the house.

THE SECRET BIRTHDAY MESSAGE

Author
Eric Carle

Illustrator
Eric Carle

Publisher
HarperCollins, 1972

Pages
18

Other Books by Carle
The Very Hungry Caterpillar: Do You Want to Be My Friend?; The Mixed-Up Chameleon; The Tiny Seed; 1,2,3 to the Zoo; The Grouchy Ladybug; Have You Seen My Cat?; A House for Hermit Crab; I See a Song; Pancakes, Pancakes!; The Very Quiet Cricket

Summary
Tim finds his birthday present, a puppy, by following the directions in a secret message. Matching shapes, recognizing patterns, and learning about following directions are among the skills children can practice through this book.

Introduction
Do you like surprises? Do you like birthday surprises? Tell us about a birthday present you would really like to receive. *After discussion:* We are going to read a story together about a boy named Tim whose birthday is full of surprises. It all begins with a secret message (show children the first page with text). Let's find out what the message says.

Discussion Questions

1 What did Tim find under his pillow the night before his birthday? (He found a strange envelope.)

2 What did Tim have to do to find his birthday present? (He had to follow the directions given in the secret message.)

3 Why do you think Tim had to find his birthday gift rather than someone just giving it to him? (Answers may vary.)

4 Would you like to get a secret message to get your birthday present(s)? (Answers may vary.)

5 Who do you think gave Tim the secret message and the birthday present? (Answers may vary.)

6 Which of your birthdays have you liked the most? Explain. (Answers may vary.)

7 Do you think the puppy was a good birthday gift? Why or why not? (Answers may vary.)

From *Read It Again! Pre-K Book 2*, published by GoodYearBooks. Copyright © 1994 Libby Miller and Liz Rothlein.

THE SECRET BIRTHDAY MESSAGE

ORAL LANGUAGE ACTIVITY

Directions

Using a large sheet of yellow tagboard, draw a large star, laminate it, and cut it out. Place the star on the floor in the center of the circle time area. Have the children's names printed on strips of paper and placed in a paper bag. Seat the children in a semicircle around the star.

Introduce and demonstrate the following words: on, by, around, in, above, over, below, under, and around by walking *on the star, over the star, by the star, in the star, around the star*, etc. Using the tune of "Here We Go 'Round the Mulberry Bush" and the words suggested below, pull the name of the first child out of the paper bag and sing the first verse, filling in that child's name. Continue by pulling another name card and using that name to sing the second verse as the child follows the directions.

_____ walks on the big yellow star, big yellow star, big yellow star.
_____ walks on the big yellow star all day long.

(Pick up the star so that the children can go under it.)
_____ crawls under the big yellow star, big yellow star, big yellow star.
_____ crawls under the big yellow star all day long.

_____ skips around the big yellow star, big yellow star, big yellow star.
_____ skips around the big yellow star all day long.

_____ hops over the big yellow star, big yellow star, big yellow star.
_____ hops over the big yellow star all day long.

_____ wiggles by the big yellow star, big yellow star, big yellow star.
_____ wiggles by the big yellow star all day long.

After all the verses provided have been sung, make up additional verses using other words.

_____ walks through the classroom door, classroom door, classroom door.
_____ walks through the classroom door all day long.

_____ crawls under the big round table, big round table, big round table.
_____ crawls under the big round table all day long.

LEARNING CENTER ACTIVITY

Directions

Place the "Count the Candles" activity marker (p. 75) at the center. Cut out and laminate the number cards below. (You might wish to make 2 or 3 sets.) Have the children make 9 birthday cakes out of clay. Next, have them put the numbers in order from 1 to 9. Finally, have them place the same number of candles in their birthday cakes that they see on the candle cards.

1 - one	2 - two	3 - three
4 - four	5 - five	6 - six
7 - seven	8 - eight	9 - nine

From *Read It Again! Pre-K Book 2*, published by GoodYearBooks. Copyright © 1994 Libby Miller and Liz Rothlein.

LEARNING CENTER ACTIVITY MARKER
COUNT THE CANDLES

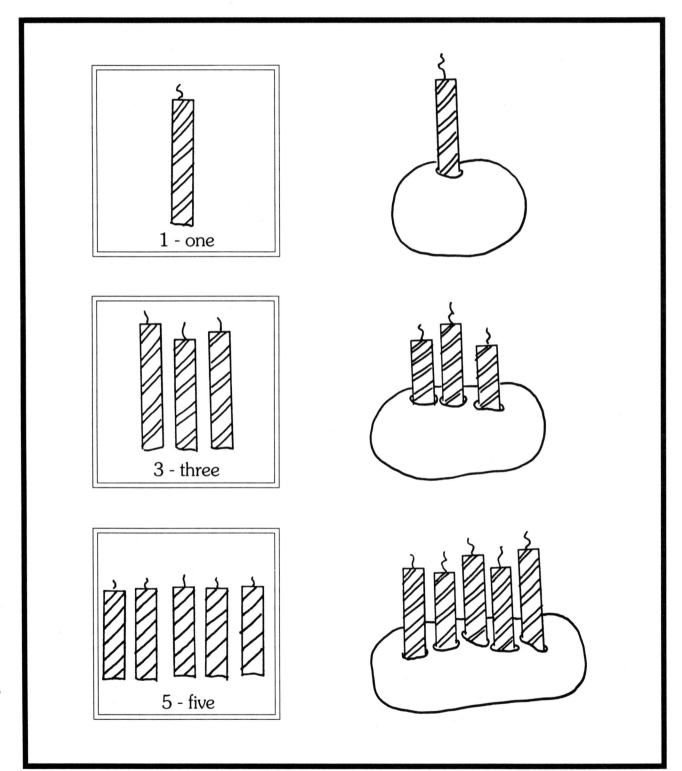

1 - one

3 - three

5 - five

Name _____ Date _____

We have been reading the book *The Secret Birthday Message* by Eric Carle. It is a story about a little boy named Tim and his birthday surprise. In this story, Tim has to follow the directions in a secret message in order to get his birthday present. To find his present he has to look *below* a star, climb *behind* a rock, go *in* a cave, look *up* and crawl *through* an opening, go *down* the stairs, walk *through* a door, and climb *up* and *through* another opening to finally get his birthday surprise.

The homework this week will emphasize positional words (on, in, over, under, etc.), listening skills, and direction-following while playing games.

Monday: Place a small stepstool or chair in an area where your child can move around easily. Then play a variation of "Simon Says." Use your name—Mommy, Daddy, Grandma, etc.—instead of Simon's name.

Give your child the following directions:
    Mommy (or Daddy) says, "Walk *around* the chair."
    Mommy says, "Sit *down* on the chair."
    Mommy says, "Go *behind* the chair."
    Continue with your own directions using the following words: *over, under, by, next to, on, beneath, up, around,* etc.

Your child should only follow those directions that include your name. If the directions do not include your name, your child should not follow the directions. Once your child is thoroughly familiar with how the game is played, let him/her give the directions.

Tuesday: Set up a maze that will allow your child to crawl *under* a table, step *up* and *over* a chair, walk *around* a stand, go *between* two chairs, etc. To make the game more challenging, you can combine two directions (for example, hop on one leg and crawl under the table, skip to the chair and then step up and over it). Tell the child that if he/she successfully completes the maze, you will follow one of his/her mazes!

From *Read It Again! Pre-K Book 2*, published by GoodYearBooks. Copyright © 1994 Libby Miller and Liz Rothlein.

Wednesday: Color and cut out the star on the attached page. Have your child use the star as he/she follows the simple one-step directions.

Put the star *under* your foot.
Put the star *over* your head.
Put the star *below* the table.
Put the star *above* the sofa.
Put the star *between* your legs.
Put the star *under* your chin.

Continue with your own one-step directions and have fun.

Thursday: Color and cut out the rock on the attached page. Have your child use the star and the rock to follow the two-step directions listed below.

Put the star *on* the table and put the rock on the floor.
Stand *on* the star and put the rock over your head.
Put the rock *between* your legs and hop three times.
Put the star *under* your bed and put the rock on the kitchen counter.

Continue with your own two-step directions.

Friday: Return the rock and the star to school for additional direction-following activities.

Parent's Signature _____

star

rock

THE SECRET BIRTHDAY MESSAGE

EVALUATION

Name _____ Date _____

ONE- AND TWO-STEP DIRECTIONS/POSITIONAL PREPOSITIONS

Directions

Use the picture of the star and the rock on page 78 to evaluate children's understanding of positional prepositions and their ability to follow one- and two-step directions.

One-Step Directions/Positional Prepositions

Tell the child to:	Does the child understand the positional prepositions?	Can the child follow one-step directions?
1. Place the star over his/her head.	Yes___ No___	Yes___ No___
2. Place the star under his/her chair.	Yes___ No___	Yes___ No___
3. Place the star between his/her legs.	Yes___ No___	Yes___ No___
4. Put the rock on the floor.	Yes___ No___	Yes___ No___
5. Put the rock next to the table.	Yes___ No___	Yes___ No___

The child understood ____/5 prepositions.

The child followed ____/5 directions.

Two-Step Directions/Prepositional Phrases

Tell the child to:	Does the child understand positional prepositions?	Is the child able to follow two-step directions?
1. Put the rock on top of the table and hold the star above your head.	Yes ___ No ___	Yes ___ No ___
2. Place the star between your knees and put the rock behind your back.	Yes ___ No ___	Yes ___ No ___
3. Place the star in front of you and put the rock under your feet.	Yes ___ No ___	Yes ___ No ___
4. Place the rock on top of the chair and put the star above the rock.	Yes ___ No ___	Yes ___ No ___
5. Place the star below your chin and put the rock next to your leg.	Yes ___ No ___	Yes ___ No ___

The child understood ___/10 prepositions/prepositional phrases.

The child followed ___/5 directions.

Child's birthday _____

Does the child know his/her birthday? Yes ___ No ___

From *Read It Again! Pre-K Book 2*, published by GoodYearBooks. Copyright © 1994 Libby Miller and Liz Rothlein.

THE SECRET BIRTHDAY MESSAGE

Additional Activities

1 The Secret Message

Write the secret message from Eric Carle's *The Secret Birthday Message* on the chalkboard. Re-read it together and talk about how it is written. Then, as a group, create a secret message to send to another class or group of children. To do this, the group will need to determine what they want to hide, where to hide it, and then plan a route to get there.

2 The Card Shop

Talk with the children about their birthdays and the special cards they have received. If possible, have them bring in some birthday cards. Together, discuss why it is fun to get cards. List their reasons on the chalkboard. Then have them design their own birthday cards for Tim. Make the following supplies available: white paper, construction paper, markers, crayons, paint, glitter, etc. When the outside of the cards are complete, they can write birthday messages inside. Allow time to share the cards.

3 Birthday Book

When celebrating a student's birthday in the classroom, staple several pages of plain paper between a construction paper cover. Write "Happy Birthday" plus the child's name on the cover. Have the child's classmates draw pictures or write birthday wishes in the book. Send the book home as a memento of the birthday celebration.

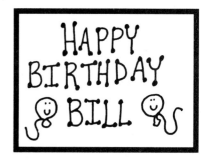

4 Tim's Birthday Cookies

In *The Secret Birthday Message,* Tim receives a birthday present but he doesn't have a birthday party. Help Tim celebrate his birthday by creating a party for him and making cookies using the following recipe:

 1 cup peanut butter
 1/2 cup sugar
 2 eggs

Mix the ingredients together until smooth and creamy. Drop by a teaspoon on an ungreased cookie sheet and bake at 350° for 8–10 minutes.

Don't forget to sing "Happy Birthday" to Tim as you eat the cookies.

THE SECRET BIRTHDAY MESSAGE

5 Birthday Graph

Make a graph with the names of the months written across the bottom. Give everyone a piece of paper that is the same size as one of the boxes in your graph. Have each child write his/her name on the paper. Then help children place their papers in the appropriate column.

					Leon	Beth					
					Maria	Jorge					
Jan.	Feb.	March	April	May	June	July	Aug.	Sept.	Oct.	Nov.	Dec.

Use the graph to make comparisons. Which month has the most birthdays? Which month has the least? Is there a month with no birthdays? Which months have the same number of birthdays?

6 Happy Birthday Center

Create a "Happy Birthday Center" where a calendar of everyone's birthday is displayed plus books that relate to birthdays such as:

The Happy Birthday Present by Joan Heilbroner (HarperCollins, 1961).
A Birthday Present for Mama by Nicole Lorian (Random House, 1984).
The Surprise Party by Annabelle Prager (Pantheon Books, 1977).
A Letter to Amy by Ezra Jack Keats (HarperCollins, 1968).

Children can help decorate this center by bringing in birthday party favors, streamers, and pictures and posters pertaining to birthdays, etc. If the area is large enough, it could be used as a place to celebrate birthdays of the children in the class.

7 A Mulberry Birthday

One of the most important days of the year in the life of a child is his/her birthday. Copy the song on page 83 and use it to help children learn their birthdates. Write the child's name in the title of the song and add the child's birthdate and age in the appropriate blanks.

From *Read It Again! Pre-K Book 2*, published by GoodYearBooks. Copyright © 1994 Libby Miller and Liz Rothlein.

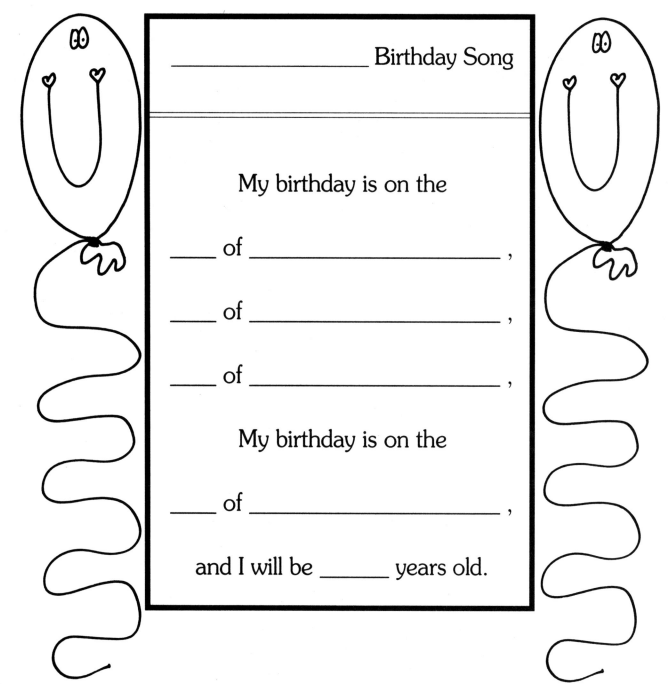

_____ Birthday Song

My birthday is on the

____ of _____ ,

____ of _____ ,

____ of _____ ,

My birthday is on the

____ of _____ ,

and I will be _____ years old.

8 The Secret "S" Flap Book

Day 1: Read *The Secret Birthday Message* and then make a list of the positional words found in the story (below, behind, in, up, through, down). Make a rebus to illustrate the words or use the pictures on pages 87 to 88 to illustrate these concepts.

Day 2: Cluster the words that begin like "secret." Write each word and label it with a picture. Use the cluster as a resource for the flap book.

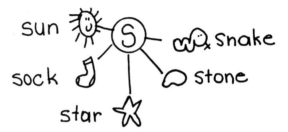

Day 3: Review the positional words found in the story. Select the word "behind" and demonstrate its meaning using concrete objects. Then begin construction of the "Secret S Flap Book." Here is what to do:

1. Fold a piece of 12" x 18" manila paper in half (Figure A).
2. Draw a curved line about halfway down from the open side to the fold (Figure A from number 1 to 2).
3. Cut on the curved line and up the fold to the top of the paper (Figure A).
4. Draw a *big* rock under the curved line and color it (Figure B).
5. Complete the sentence "The s__ is behind the rock." (found in the box on page 86) with an "s" word from the cluster.
6. Cut out the sentence and glue it inside the rock (Figure C).
7. Draw a picture of an "s" word inside (Figure D).

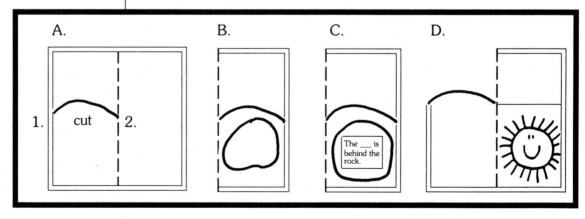

A. B. C. D.

1. cut 2.

The ___ is behind the rock.

From *Read It Again! Pre-K Book 2*, published by GoodYearBooks. Copyright © 1994 Libby Miller and Liz Rothlein.

THE SECRET BIRTHDAY MESSAGE

Day 4: Once again, review the positional words from *The Secret Birthday Message*. Add additional positional words to the list, including the word *under*. Follow the same directions as on Day 2 by demonstrating the meaning of the word and using an "s" word from the cluster. Follow the directions below for the flap book.

1. Fold an 8" x 4" piece of paper in half (to make a 4" x 4" square). Attach the folded paper to paper E in the position in the diagram to the right. Have the children draw a picture of a bed on the folded piece of paper.
2. Have the children draw an "s" picture under the flap.
3. Complete the sentence "The <u>s</u>_ is under the bed." on page 86. Cut out the sentence and glue it to the bottom of Figure F.

E.

F.

Day 5:
1. Make an envelope by stapling an 8" x 4" square of paper as shown in Figure G.
2. Decorate the square to look like wrapping paper (Figure H).
3. Punch a hole at the top of a piece of 3" x 4" paper (Figure I), and help children attach a loop made of yarn through it.
4. Have the children select one of the "s" words from the cluster and illustrate it on the paper.
5. Help children complete the sentence "The s_____ is in the present" from page 86. Ask them to cut out the sentence and glue it to the top of a piece of paper (Figure J).
6. Slip the "s" word picture into it (Figure K).
7. Put the completed pages together to make a book!

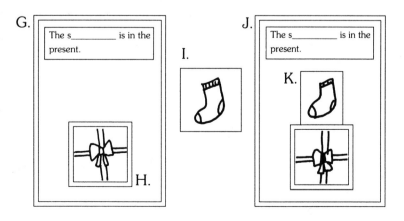

From *Read It Again! Pre-K Book 2*, published by GoodYearBooks. Copyright © 1994 Libby Miller and Liz Rothlein.

Use the sentences below with Activity Number 8: The Secret "S" Flap Book activity.

DAY 3:

> # The s_____
> ## is behind the rock.

DAY 4:

> # The s_____
> ## is under the bed.

DAY 5:

> # The s_____
> ## is in the present.

9 Make a Wish

Traditionally, a person makes a wish before blowing out all the candles on his/her birthday cake. If all the candles are blown out, the wish is supposed to come true. If all the candles are not blown out, the wish doesn't come true.

After reading *The Secret Birthday Message,* have the children close their eyes and imagine the present that they would like to receive. Tell the children to keep the surprise a secret. Using a 12" x 18" piece of manila paper, have children draw a picture illustrating what they would wish for. Help them print the following sentence underneath: "I would wish for a _____ for my birthday present."

ball

I would wish for a _____ for my birthday present.

under

in

between

behind

down

over

up

through

SNOW MAGIC

Author
Harriet Ziefert

Illustrator
Claire Schumacher

Publisher
Viking Penguin, Inc., 1988

Pages
33

Other Books by Ziefert
Clean House for Mole & Mouse; Dark Night; Sleepy Night; Harry Takes a Bath; Jason's Bus Ride; Mike & Tony: Best Friends; New Coat for Anna; New House for Mole & Mouse; Nicky Upstairs & Down; Pet Day; Sleepy Dog

From *Read It Again! Pre-K Book 2*, published by GoodYearBooks. Copyright © 1994 Libby Miller and Liz Rothlein.

Summary
The snow falls all night long, and by morning the whole countryside is covered with a deep blanket of snow. Then, one by one, the snow people appear and have a party to celebrate the first snow on the first day of winter.

Introduction
What does snow look like? How does it feel? We are going to read a story about the first snow of the winter. What do you think will happen during this first snow? (Note: For children living in areas without wintry seasons, pose all questions as "What do you think?," such as "What do you think snow looks like?")

Discussion Questions

1 Describe how the snow women, snow men, and snow children looked. Where do you think they came from? (Answers may vary.)

2 What were the snow people carrying in their boxes and bags? (Answers may vary, but might include: food, decorations, and other things needed for a party.)

3 Do you think they selected a good place to have their party? Why or why not? (Answers may vary.)

4 Why did they have a party? (Because the first snow of the year fell on the first day of winter.) What are some reasons for you and your friends/family to have a party? (Answers may vary, but might include birthdays, holidays, and other special occasions.)

5 Would you like to go to the snow people's party? Why or why not? (Answers may vary.)

6 What did the snow people do at the party? (They cheered, ate, danced, and sang.) Can you think of anything else they might have done at the party? (Answers may vary.)

Materials: Chart paper or chalkboard

Activity

As you sing the song below to the tune of "The Farmer in the Dell," illustrate each verse on a large sheet of chart paper or the chalkboard.

There's snow upon the ground.
There's snow upon the ground.
Hi!, Ho! It's cold outside!
There's snow upon the ground.

There's a snowman in the snow.
There's a snowman in the snow.
Hi!, Ho! It's cold outside!
There's a snowman in the snow.

The snowman has a hat.
The snowman has a hat.
Hi!, Ho! It's cold outside!
The snowman has a hat.

The snowman has a nose.
The snowman has a nose.
Hi!, Ho! It's cold outside!
The snowman has a nose.

The snowman has two eyes.
The snowman has two eyes.
Hi!, Ho! It's cold outside!
The snowman has two eyes.

The snowman has a mouth.
The snowman has a mouth.
Hi!, Ho! It's cold outside!
The snowman has a mouth.

The snowman has two arms.
The snowman has two arms.
Hi!, Ho! It's cold outside!
The snowman has two arms.

The snowman has a scarf.
The snowman has a scarf.
Hi!, Ho! It's cold outside!
The snowman has a scarf.

The snowman has big shoes.
The snowman has big shoes.
Hi!, Ho! It's cold outside!
The snowman has big shoes.

From *Read It Again! Pre-K Book 2*, published by GoodYearBooks. Copyright © 1994 Libby Miller and Liz Rothlein.

Materials: Place the "Make a Snow Person Center" learning center activity marker (p. 92) at the learning center. Make the following materials available at the "Make a Snow Person Center": large sheets of white paper, crayons and/or markers, wallpaper samples for a scarf and hat, glue, and scissors.

Activity

Give each child at the center a large sheet of paper on which to make a snow person. Then have children follow the directions on the center marker (page 92). When their snow people are complete, have the children cut them out and add them to the snow people mural.

Mural

Using a large sheet of paper or rolled paper, have children work together to paint a snowy background for the snow people using white paint.

LEARNING CENTER ACTIVITY MARKER

MAKE A SNOW PERSON CENTER

Make 3 circles.

Make a funny hat.

Make 2 eyes.

Make 1 mouth.

Make 1 nose.

Make 2 arms.

Make 1 scarf.

Make 2 shoes.

Cut out the snow person and put it on the snow mural.

PARENT BULLETIN/HOMEWORK

Name _____ Date _____

We have been reading *Snow Magic* by Harriet Ziefert. It is a story about snow falling all night long and by morning the whole countryside is covered with a deep blanket of snow. Then, one by one, the snow people appear and have a party to celebrate the first snow on the first day of winter.

Your child is going to make his/her own snowy day book for homework this week. To make the book you will need 4 pieces of white paper (all the same size), crayons or markers, scissors, glue, a stapler, and the following directions:

A. Cut out sentence number 1 from the poem below on the dotted line and glue to the bottom of one sheet of white paper.

B. Have your child illustrate the picture in the space above the sentence. **Have your child outline the picture with a black crayon and color it in.**

1. Snow in the wintertime falls on my hat.

2. Snow in the wintertime falls on my cat.

3. Snow in the wintertime falls on my tree.

4. Snow in the wintertime falls on me.

Ask your child to make another page for sentence 2 on Tuesday, a third page for sentence 3 on Wednesday, and a page for sentence 4 on Thursday. Staple the pages together to make a book. Help your child remember to bring the book back to school on Friday.

Parent's Signature_____

EVALUATION

Name _____ Date _____

Directions
Use the poem from the Parent Bulletin for the weekly evaluation. Have each child read his/her homework poem. Use the poem for a running record of the child's reading (or memorizing).

> Snow in the wintertime falls on my hat.
>
> Snow in the wintertime falls on my cat.
>
> Snow in the wintertime falls on my tree.
>
> Snow in the wintertime falls on me.

Hand the child his/her homework poem. Ask the child to read the words and point to each as he/she reads it.

1. Is the child able to "read" the sentences? Yes___ No___
(Remember, reading at this level is likely to mean that the child has memorized the sentences.)

2. Does the child match the spoken word to the written word? Yes ___ No___

3. Do the child's illustrations match the sentence? Yes___ No___

4. Can the child point to the beginning of the sentence? Yes ___ No ___

5. Can the child point to the end of the sentence? Yes ___ No ___

6. Can the child find the word "cat"? Yes ___ No___

7. Can the child find the word "tree"? Yes ___ No ___

8. Can the child find the word "snow"? Yes ___ No ___

9. Can the child find the word "winter"? Yes ___ No ___

From *Read It Again! Pre-K Book 2*, published by GoodYearBooks. Copyright © 1994 Libby Miller and Liz Rothlein.

SNOW MAGIC

Additional Activities

1 Melting Time

Fill a clear plastic glass half full with ice cubes or snow. Then ask children to predict how long it will take to melt and how much water they predict there will be. Write their predictions on the chalkboard and make a mark on the glass to show how much water there will be. Encourage children to observe what happens to the ice/snow over the next few hours. Once the ice/snow is melted, record the amount of time it took and compare this with their predictions. Talk together about how closely they were able to predict the amount of water.

If possible, as an additional experience, fill one cup half full with ice cubes and the other with snow. Then ask the children to predict which will melt first and why. Which will produce the most water?

2 Snow Cones

Make snow cones for a snack by packing cleaned crushed ice in a paper cup. Then pour fruit juice, fruit flavored gelatin, or flavored syrup over the ice.

3 Snow Library

Provide an assortment of other books related to snow such as *Katy and the Big Snow* by Virginia Lee Burton (Houghton Mifflin, 1973); *White Snow, Bright Snow* by Alvin Tresselt (Lothrop, 1947); *The Snowman* by Raymond Briggs (Random House, 1978); *The Big Snow* by Berta and Elmer Hader (Macmillan, 1948); *Sadie and the Snowman* by Allen Morgan (Scholastic, 1987); and *Our Snowman* by M. B. Goffstein (HarperCollins, 1986). The books could be placed on a table or shelf that has been covered with cotton batting to represent snow. You may even want to add paper snowflakes, hung from the ceiling, to represent snow falling.

4 Snow Pictures

Give each child a piece of black construction paper and a sheet of white paper. Tell children to make a snow scene by tearing shapes from the white paper to represent snowflakes, a snow person, a snow-covered hill, etc. These shapes should be pasted on the black paper. Display the finished pictures.

5 Marshmallow Snow People

Help children make marshmallow snow people by following these directions:

1. Join two large marshmallows together with a toothpick to form the head and body.
2. Break another toothpick in half and use the pieces for arms.
3. Stick small marshmallows on to these toothpicks.
4. Push small black pieces of licorice into the marshmallows to make eyes and a nose; use "red hots" for the mouth.
5. Make a hat from black construction paper.
6. Allow the children to eat the extra marshmallows.

6 Snow Story

Discuss with the children all the things they can do in the snow. Create a web around the word "snow," similar to the one below, writing the children's comments as they are offered. Illustrate.

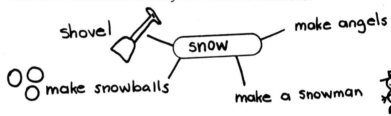

Then write on the board or on chart paper the following cloze sentence: "I can _____ in the snow." As a group, write and illustrate a story about one or a combination of things they like to do in the snow. This story might be written on chart paper that has been cut in round circles to represent snowballs or you may wish to use the activity sheet on page 99 so that each child has a page in a class book.

7 Rice Pictures

Provide each child with a piece of black construction paper, glue and some rice. Tell everyone to draw an outline for a snowperson on the black paper and then spread glue on one small section at a time. Cover that section with rice. Children should continue with the glue and rice until the entire snow person shape is covered. Scraps of colorful construction paper may be used to make eyes nose, mouth, buttons, scarf and so on for the snow person.

8 Snow Magic Phonics Book

Brainstorm with children all the words they can think of that begin with the sound of "s" as in "snowy" or "snowman." Write the following cloze sentence on the blackboard: "I see a s_____ on a snowy day." Give each child a copy of the activity on page 100. Using the

From *Read It Again! Pre-K Book 2*, published by GoodYearBooks. Copyright © 1994 Libby Miller and Liz Rothlein.

pictures from the web (Activity 6), have the children fill in the blank at the bottom of the page and illustrate their sentence.

9 White on Black

Provide children with a section of the newspaper (black and white page) and a sheet of plain white paper. Ask them to make a snow scene on the newspaper by tearing the white sheet into desired shapes (circles for snowmen, odd shapes for snowflakes, and so on).

10 Garbage Bag Snow People

Materials: Two small white garbage bags, newspaper, yarn, construction paper, glue, and clear adhesive tape for each child.

Activity:

Put one garbage bag inside the other so that the newspaper will not show through. Fill about one-third of the bag with crumpled newspaper. Next, tie some yarn around the bag tightly to make a head. Fill the rest of the bag with crumpled newspaper. Then tie yarn around the bottom to secure the bag shut. Finally, use construction paper to make a hat, eyes, nose, mouth, and buttons. Glue or tape them to the snow people.

Have children tell or write stories about their snow people.

11 Soap Snowballs

Materials: Ivory Snow® Flakes, water, mixing bowl, measuring cup, tin foil, cookie sheet.

Ingredients: 4 cups of Ivory Snow® Flakes and 1/2 cup of water.

Activity

Add small amounts of water to the Ivory Snow® Flakes and mix. Continue mixing until the soap pulls away from the sides of the bowl and forms a ball. Give each child a small amount (2 teaspoons) of the soap mixture. Tell everyone to roll the soap into a pretend snowball. Put the soap snowballs on foil on the cookie sheet and allow them to dry for about one week. As a group, write a short story about their snowballs. When the snowballs are dry, the children can take them home and use as a bath soap. They will notice that these snowballs gradually melt away in the water. Food coloring may be added to the "snowballs." When dry, they may be used as crayons to write in the bathtub.

12 Bird Feeders
Materials: Cheerios®, yarn.

Activity
Give each child a length of string on which
to lace Cheerios®. Have the children hang the
Cheerios® bird feeder on a tree.

13 Pine Cone Feeders
Materials: Pine cones, peanut butter, birdseed,
plastic knives, string, plastic bags.

Activity
Have children first spread peanut butter on pine cones using a plastic
knife and then roll them in birdseed. Attach a string. Place the covered
ones in plastic bags for the trip home. Children can hang their bird
feeders in trees in their yards.

14 Snowman(woman), Snowman(woman), Touch the Ground
Repeat the following chant as the children do the actions (substitute
"snowwoman" or "snow person" if you like):

> Snowman, snowman, nod your head.
> Snowman, snowman, go to bed.
>
> Snowman, snowman, wink your eye.
> Snowman, snowman, jump up high.
>
> Snowman, snowman, touch your knee.
> Snowman, snowman, sit quietly.
>
> Snowman, snowman, bend way down.
> Snowman, snowman, melt to the ground.

Have the children pretend to be a snowman. Have them brainstorm
additional actions that they might do as a snowman.

From *Read It Again! Pre-K Book 2*, published by GoodYearBooks. Copyright © 1994 Libby Miller and Liz Rothlein.

I can _____
in the snow.

I see a s _____
on a snowy day.

THE VERY BUSY SPIDER

Author
Eric Carle

Illustrator
Eric Carle

Publisher
Philomel Books, 1989

Pages
23

Other Books by Carle
Do You Want to Be My Friend?; The Grouchy Ladybug; Have You Seen My Cat?; A House for a Hermit Crab; The Mixed-Up Chameleon; 1,2,3, to The Zoo; Rooster's Off to See the World; The Secret Birthday Message; The Tiny Seed; The Very Hungry Caterpillar

Summary

On a sunny morning, a spider begins to spin a web on a fencepost in a farmyard. One by one, the farm animals try to divert the spider's attention, but she sticks to her task, and readers can see as well as feel the web as it grows. The completed web is not only beautiful, but useful, too. The spider uses it to catch a pesty fly that appears again and again in the illustrations throughout the book.

Introduction

Tell children that this story is about a spider who is so busy and interested in spinning her web that she doesn't let any of the farm animals interfere with what she is doing. Ask children to tell about times when they have been busy like the spider and didn't want to be bothered. What were they doing? What happened?

Discussion Questions

1 Who were some of the animals that talked with the spider and what did they say? (Horse: neigh; cow: moo; sheep: baa; goat: maa; pig: oink; dog: woof; cat: meow; duck: quack; rooster: cock-a-doodle-do.)

2 Do you think the spider would have done any of the things the farm animals asked her to do even if she wasn't so busy spinning a web? Why or why not? (Answers may vary.)

3 Some of the things that happened in this story were real and others were make-believe. What is one real thing that happened in the story? (Spiders spin webs; flies get caught in webs.) What is one make-believe thing that happened? (The animals talked.)

4 How do you think the farm animals felt when the spider didn't answer them? (Answers may vary.)

5 What do you do when you see a spider web? Why? (Answers may vary.)

6 Let's look carefully at the pictures of the barnyard animals. Can you find the pesty fly on each one? Show us where.

ORAL LANGUAGE ACTIVITY

Directions

If you are using a flannelboard, use pages 103 and 104 as patterns for making flannel spider parts.

If you are using a magnetic board, color the spider parts on pages 103 and 104. Cut out the parts and laminate them. Then place magnetic strips on the back of each part and place them on your board.

Materials: Magnetic chalkboard or flannelboard, spider parts on pages 103–104, magnetic tape, markers or crayons. (If you don't have a magnetized chalkboard, a metal cookie sheet will work.)

Activity

Sing the following song about spiders to the tune of "The Farmer in the Dell." As you sing the song, use the flannel or magnetic spider parts to emphasize the verses.

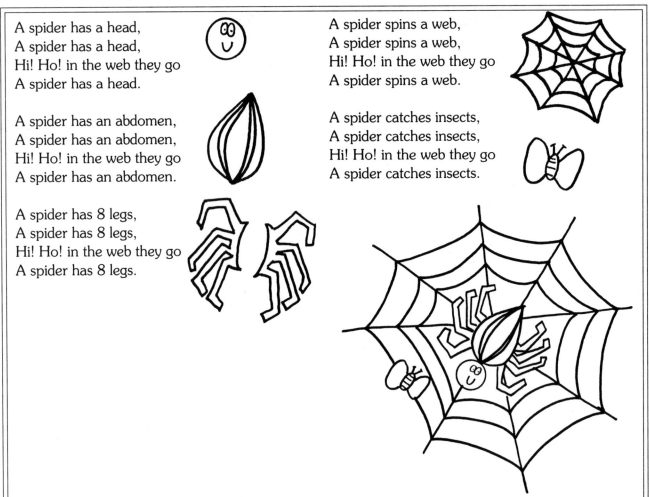

A spider has a head,
A spider has a head,
Hi! Ho! in the web they go
A spider has a head.

A spider has an abdomen,
A spider has an abdomen,
Hi! Ho! in the web they go
A spider has an abdomen.

A spider has 8 legs,
A spider has 8 legs,
Hi! Ho! in the web they go
A spider has 8 legs.

A spider spins a web,
A spider spins a web,
Hi! Ho! in the web they go
A spider spins a web.

A spider catches insects,
A spider catches insects,
Hi! Ho! in the web they go
A spider catches insects.

From *Read It Again! Pre-K Book 2*, published by GoodYearBooks. Copyright © 1994 Libby Miller and Liz Rothlein.

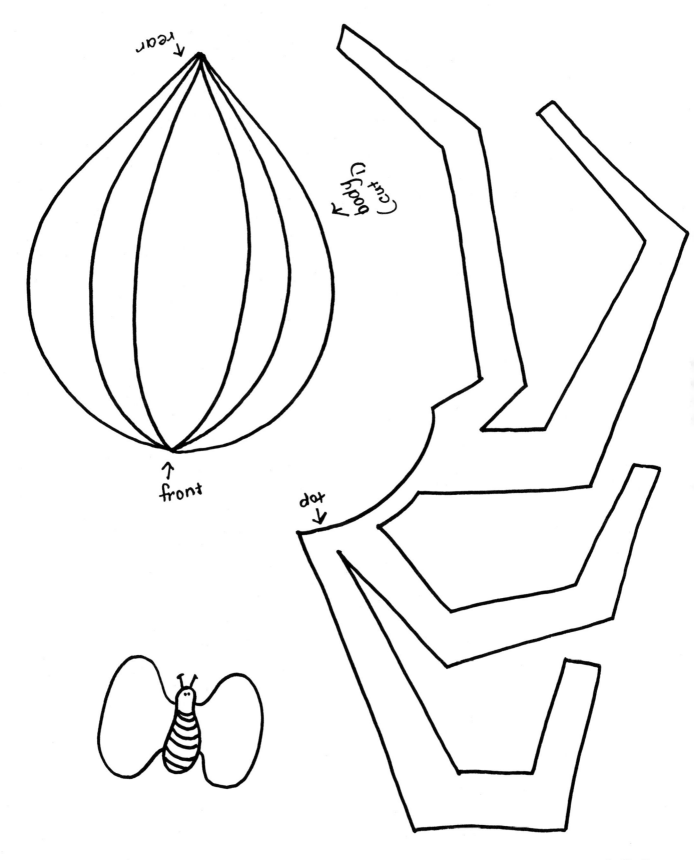

rear

body
(cut)

front

dot

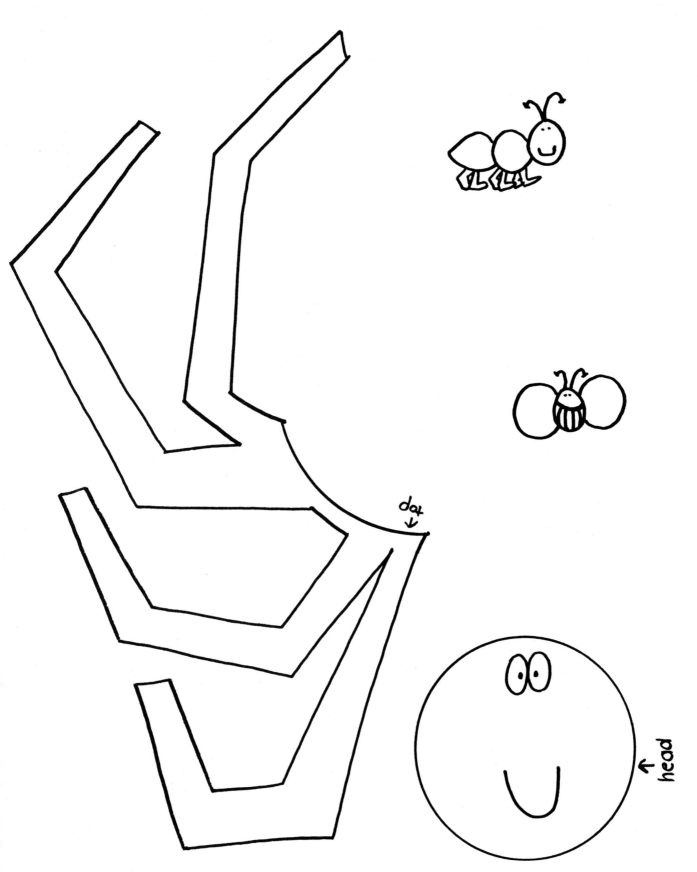

dot
↓

head
↑

Directions
Place the "Spider's Sorting Center" activity marker (p. 106) at the learning center.

Make copies of the pictures below and those on pages 107 and 108. Color the pictures, glue them to a sheet of cardboard, laminate, and cut them apart. Put the picture pieces in a small box. Provide two additional boxes for sorting the pictures. Cover one box with green paper and write, **"Animals that were in the farmyard."** Cover the other box with red paper and write, **"Animals that were not in the farmyard."** Then ask the children to recall all the animals that were in the farmyard with the spider and sort the pictures accordingly.

Note: Make an answer key by copying the pictures below and on pages 107 and 108. Draw a green circle around the pictures showing animals in the farmyard and a red circle around the pictures showing animals *not* in the farmyard.

LEARNING CENTER ACTIVITY MARKER
Spider's Sorting Center

Animals that <u>were</u> in the farmyard.

Animals that <u>were not</u> in the farmyard.

PARENT BULLETIN/HOMEWORK

Name _____ Date _____

We are reading *The Very Busy Spider* by Eric Carle. This is a story about a spider who is so busy and interested in spinning her web that she doesn't let any of the farm animals in the barnyard interfere with what she is doing. The animals that speak to the spider include a horse, cow, sheep, goat, pig, dog, cat, duck, and rooster. The following activities will help reinforce recognition of words and beginning sounds.

Monday: Have your child color the animals on the attached pages. Glue the pages to a piece of cardboard (a cereal box will work, too). Cut the pieces apart and put them in a small box or locking plastic bag.

Tuesday and Wednesday: Mix up the animal pieces. Have your child choose an animal and say the animal name, emphasizing the beginning sound. Have your child look at the word cards to find the word that starts with the sound that is heard at the beginning of the word. Help your child match the animal tc the word. If the match is correct, the two pieces will fit together.

Thursday: Hold the word card up and have your child find the animal that matches it.

Friday: Have your child bring his/her word cards to school.

Parent's Signature _____

rooster

pig

goat

cow

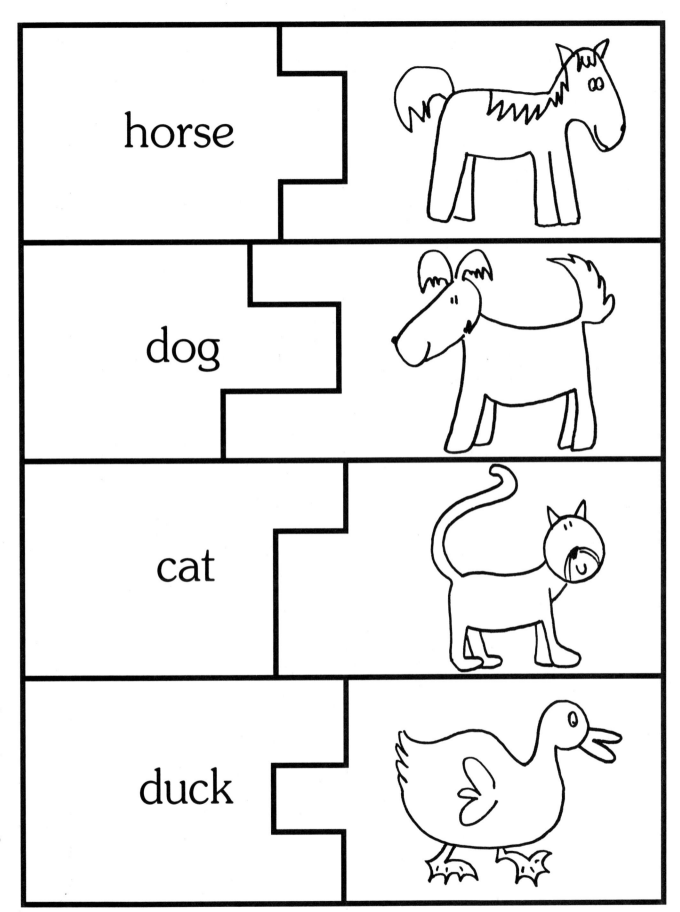

horse

dog

cat

duck

1. Give the child a copy of *The Very Busy Spider*. Read the first page to the child. Then have the child read the next 4 pages.

   a. Is the child able to "read" the pages from the book?
   Yes_____ No_____

   b. Does the child match the spoken word to the written word when pointing? Yes_____ No_____

> # The spider didn't answer. She was very busy spinning her web.

2. Use the refrain (in the above box) for the following:

   a. Can the child "read" the words in the box? Yes_____ No_____

   b. Can the child find the word *spider* and draw a circle around it?
   Yes_____ No_____

   c. Can the child find the word *web* and draw a line under it?
   Yes_____ No_____

3. Is the child able to identify words that begin with the same sound? Say the words below to the child. Check the pair of words that the child is able to identify as having the same beginning sound.

   a. spider - spider _____   b. spider - sock _____

   c. spider - book _____   d. spider - sun _____

   e. spider - cow _____   f. spider - shirt _____

   g. spider - sneaker _____   h. spider - door _____

THE VERY BUSY SPIDER

Additional Activities

1 Spider Hats

Materials:

    a. legs: 8 strips of 12" x 1" strips of paper

    b. head: 6" x 6" piece of construction paper

    c. headband: Sentence strips or pieces of paper large enough to fit around a child's head (approximately 3" x 24")

Activity

    a. legs: Fold the spider legs accordion style (Figure A).

    b. head: Draw a "big bump" on the 6" x 6" square for the spider's head (Figure B). Cut along the line. Add eyes and mouth.

    c. spider: Attach legs and head to sentence strip (Figure C).

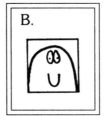

2 Farm Animal Pins

Materials: animal crackers, shellac, white glue, jewelry pins.

Activity

Shellac animal crackers and let dry. Attach pins with white glue.

3 "Eensie Weensie Spider"

As a group, repeat the traditional nursery rhyme, "The Eensie Weensie Spider." Include the actions.

> The eensie weensie spider crawled up the waterspout.
> Down came the rain and washed the spider out.
> Out came the sun and dried up all the rain.
> So the eensie weensie spider went up the spout again.

Discuss the meaning of the following vocabulary words: eensie weensie, waterspout, crawled. Make a waterspout by rolling a long sheet of butcher paper into a tube. Place in the corner of the room. Have children make spiders to wrap around the spout.

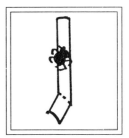

4 What We Know About Spiders

Use the K-W-L learning strategy (as illustrated below) to find out what children know about spiders. Make three columns on a chalkboard or on a large sheet of butcher paper. Label the columns with the following headings: K (what we know), W (what we want to learn), L (what we learned).

Begin by asking the children what they know about spiders. List their responses under the K column. Then ask the children what they want to learn about spiders and list their questions under the W heading.

K	W	L
WHAT WE KNOW ABOUT SPIDERS	WHAT WE WANT TO LEARN ABOUT SPIDERS	WHAT WE LEARNED ABOUT SPIDERS

Read aloud informational books about spiders. The following are excellent choices:

A New True Book: Spiders by Illa Podendorf. (Childrens Press, 1982).

Spiders Are Special Animals (Big Book) by Fred and Jeanne Biddulph. (The Wright Group, 1992).

After reading these and other books, have the children list the facts that they have just learned about spiders in the L column. Compare this list with the statements they made in the K list. Do some facts appear on both lists? Does anything in the L column contradict what appears in the K column?

THE VERY BUSY SPIDER

5 Spider Shape Fact Book

Materials: spider book shape on page 116, 8 strips of construction paper for legs, wiggle eyes.

Activity

1. Use page 116 as a pattern for the spider book. Use construction paper for the cover of the book and newsprint for the inside pages. Cut out enough pages so that each child has his/her own page for the book.
2. Use the information gathered in completing column L of the K-W-L activity as the spider facts for the book. Have each child select one of the facts from the list. Write the appropriate information at the bottom of each child's page and ask him/her to illustrate it.
3. Put the pages together to make a spider facts book.

6 The Very Busy Spider Visits the Zoo

Take a pretend trip to the zoo with the very busy spider. Write a new version of *The Very Busy Spider* using zoo animals. Use the original book as a model for the innovation. Make a list of zoo animals, the sounds that they make, and what they want to do. Have children work in pairs to illustrate. Put together to make a class book.

Examples:

Zoo Animals	Zoo Animal Sounds	Zoo Animal Activity
Lion	Gr-r-r	Want to chase a giraffe?
Monkey	Eeek, Eeek	Want to swing in a tree?
Elephant	Trumpet, Trumpet	Want to throw some dirt?

To make the spider web illustrations, drop yellow food coloring into white glue and mix. Have the children trace the spider web with a pencil and then draw over the lines with the glue mixture. The glue, when dry, will be raised up just like the web in the *The Very Busy Spider* book.

7 "Spin, Spider, Spin"

Obtain a copy of the cassette/record entitled "Spin, Spider, Spin" by Patty Zeitlin and Marcia Berman (Educational Activities). Have the children move to the music as they pretend to spin a web.

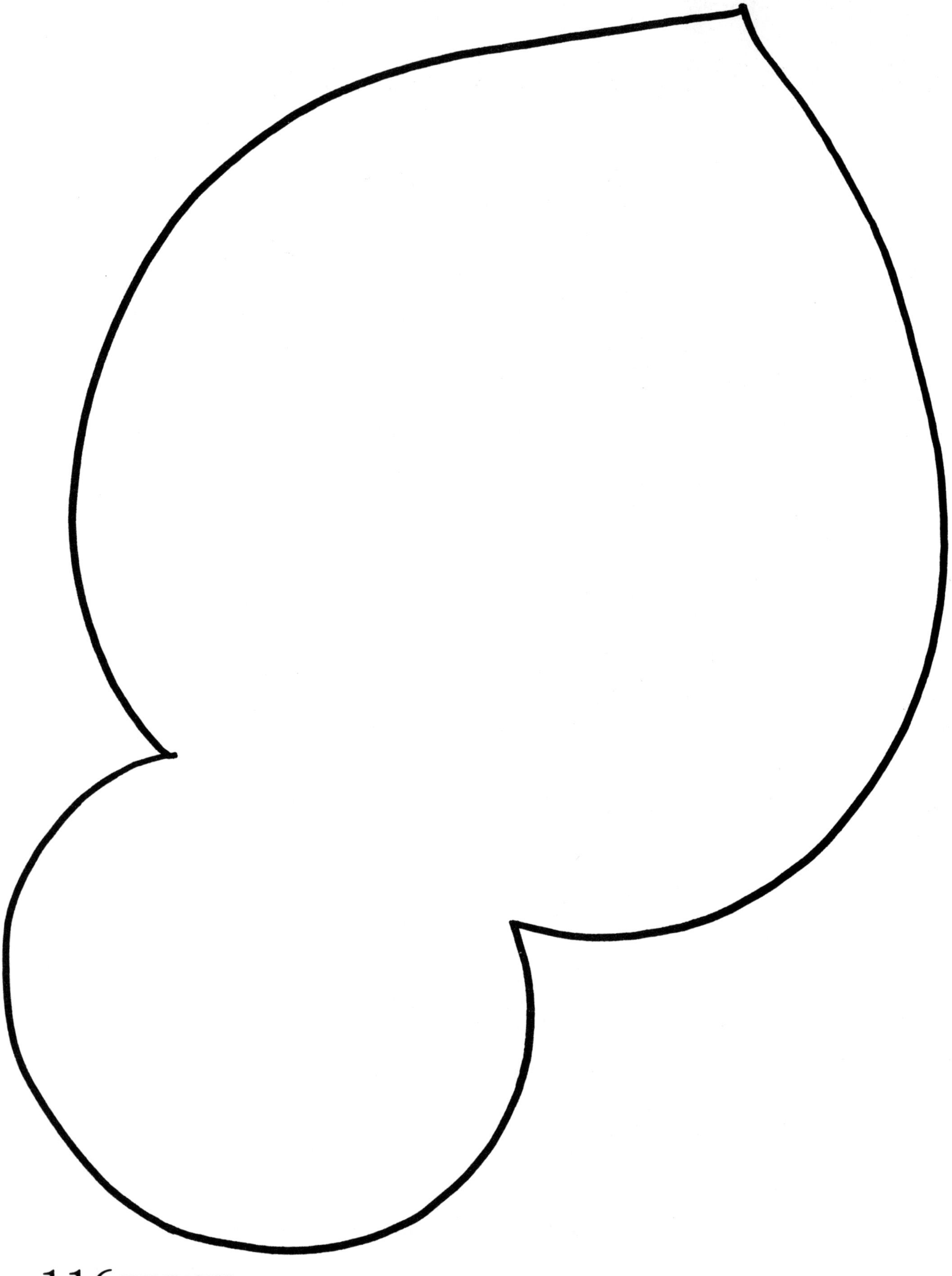

THE VERY BUSY SPIDER

8 Spider Hunt

Materials: misting bottle filled with water, Spider Hunt sheet (page 118), pencils.

Go on a walk to look for spiders and spider webs. There are many different kinds of spiders; some spiders are helpful while others are poisonous (such as the black widow or brown recluse). Emphasize that children should never touch spiders.

Use a misting bottle to lightly mist a spider web. (Misting will help to make it easier to see the web.) Have the children record what they see on their Spider Record sheet. Have children observe how spider webs are alike and how they are different.

9 Little Miss Muffet

Materials: small pillows for children to sit on (tuffets), cottage cheese mixed with fruit (curds and whey), spider hat from Activity 1, a copy of Raymond Briggs's *The Mother Goose Treasury* (Dell, 1986).

Props: Small cushion for tuffet, spider hat (from Activity 1) for the spider.

Activities
1. Copy "Little Miss Muffet" from the book onto a large sheet of chart paper. Encourage the children to read the rhyme together as they sit on their "tuffets" eating their "curds and whey."

2. Act out the nursery rhyme, choosing one child to be Little Miss Muffet and one child to be the spider.

10 Egg Carton Spiders

Materials: empty egg cartons, black paint, pipe cleaners, wiggle eyes.

Activity
Provide children with egg-carton sections (two sections per spider). Paint the egg cartons black. Cut the pipe cleaners to size for the spiders' legs. Don't forget: you will need 8 legs for each spider. Insert the legs and glue wiggle eyes onto the head.

SPIDER HUNT ACTIVITY SHEET

Spiders	Webs

From *Read It Again! Pre-K Book 2*, published by GoodYearBooks. Copyright © 1994 Libby Miller and Liz Rothlein.

11 Fingerprint Spiders

Materials: 6" x 6" white paper, ink pad, black fine-tipped markers.

Activity
Have children draw spider webs on white paper. Make the spiders by making thumbprints using the ink pad. Place the thumbprints on the web. Add legs with the marker when the web is dry.

12 Read-Aloud Books About Spiders

Read aloud and make available other books about spiders. Your choices might include: *Be Nice To Spiders* by Margaret B. Graham (Harper & Row, 1967); *Spiders* by Lillian Bacon (National Geographic Society, 1974); or *The Spider* by Margaret Lane (Dial Books for Young Readers, 1982).

13 The Spider Sees "S" Words

Write the words "The spider sees a _____." on the chalkboard. Cluster words that begin with the sound of "s," under the sentence.

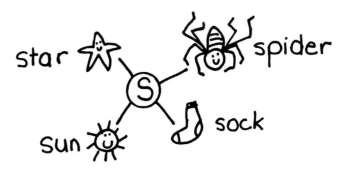

Have children choose the word they want to illustrate. Use page 120 for the illustrations. Put the pages together for a class phonics book.

The spider sees a _____ .

From *Read It Again! Pre-K Book 2*, published by GoodYearBooks. Copyright © 1994 Libby Miller and Liz Rothlein.

THE BLUE BALLOON

Author
Mick Inkpen

Illustrator
Mick Inkpen

Publisher
Little, Brown & Co., 1989

Pages
24

Other Books by Inkpen
Gumboot's Chocolatey Day; If I Had a Pig; If I Had a Sheep; One Bear at Bedtime

Summary
The Blue Balloon is the story about the adventures of a little boy and his dog. The dog finds a magical blue balloon after the little boy's birthday party. Because the balloon can expand, take on new shapes, and never breaks, it provides the little boy with exciting experiences.

Introduction
Bring in a blue balloon. After seating the children in a circle, blow up the balloon and tie a string around it. Pass the balloon around so children can examine it. Ask the children to think of things they could do with this balloon as you write them on the chalkboard. Then read *The Blue Balloon* and compare the list on the chalkboard with what the boy in the story did.

Discussion Questions

1 What would you do with a balloon if you found one? (Answers may vary.)

2 Why did the boy think it was odd that there was a blue balloon in the garden? (Because the balloons at his party were red and white.) Where do you think the blue balloon came from? (Answers may vary.)

3 Describe Kipper and the things he and the boy did together. Would you like to have a dog like Kipper? Why or why not? (Answers may vary.)

4 What did you like best about the story? Is there anything you didn't like? (Answers may vary.)

5 Do you think the little boy wanted to take Kipper on this flying trip? Why or why not? (Answers may vary.)

6 The boy said that whatever you do you should never throw a balloon away—especially if it is blue—because you never know what it will do next. What do you think the boy and the balloon will do next? (Answers may vary.)

ORAL LANGUAGE ACTIVITY

Directions

Write the words below on chart paper. The verses can be sung to the tune of "Found a Peanut." Make up hand motions to accompany the words in each verse. You may want to provide the children with blue balloons to act out the verses.

Found a blue balloon.
Found a blue balloon.
Found a blue balloon just now.
Just now I found a blue balloon.
Found a blue balloon just now.

Then I blew it up.
Then I blew it up.
Then I blew it up just now.
Just now I blew the balloon up.
Blew the balloon up just now.

Then I rubbed it.
Then I rubbed it.
Then I rubbed it just now.
Just now I rubbed the blue balloon.
Rubbed the blue balloon just now.

Then I squeezed it.
Then I squeezed it.
Then I squeezed it just now.
Just now I squeezed the blue balloon.
Squeezed the blue balloon just now.

Then I squashed it.
Then I squashed it.
Then I squashed it just now.
Just now I squashed the blue balloon.
Squashed the blue balloon just now.

Then I whacked it.
Then I whacked it.
Then I whacked it just now.
Just now I whacked the blue balloon.
Whacked the blue balloon just now.

Then I kicked it.
Then I kicked it.
Then I kicked it just now.
Just now I kicked the blue balloon.
Kicked the blue balloon just now.

Then I stretched it.
Then I stretched it.
Then I stretched it just now.
Just now I stretched the blue balloon.
Stretched the blue balloon just now.

Then it took me up.
Then it took me up.
Then it took me up just now.
Just now, it took me up and up.
It took me up and up just now.

Had a good time.
Had a good time.
Had a good time just now.
Just now I had a good time.
Had a good time just now.

From *Read It Again! Pre-K Book 2*, published by GoodYearBooks. Copyright © 1994 Libby Miller and Liz Rothlein.

Color Word Concentration

Directions

Place The Blue Balloon Center Activity Marker (page 124) at the learning center. Make two copies of the pictures on pages 125 and 126. Cut out the pictures, color, and glue them to posterboard to make playing cards. Play Concentration using the cards by following these directions:

1. Turn cards facedown.
2. Player 1 turns over two cards. If the cards match, the player may keep the cards. If the cards do not match, they are placed facedown on the playing surface.
3. Then Player 2 turns over two cards and follows the same procedures as Player 1.
4. Continue until all matches have been made.

LEARNING CENTER ACTIVITY MARKER
THE BLUE BALLOON

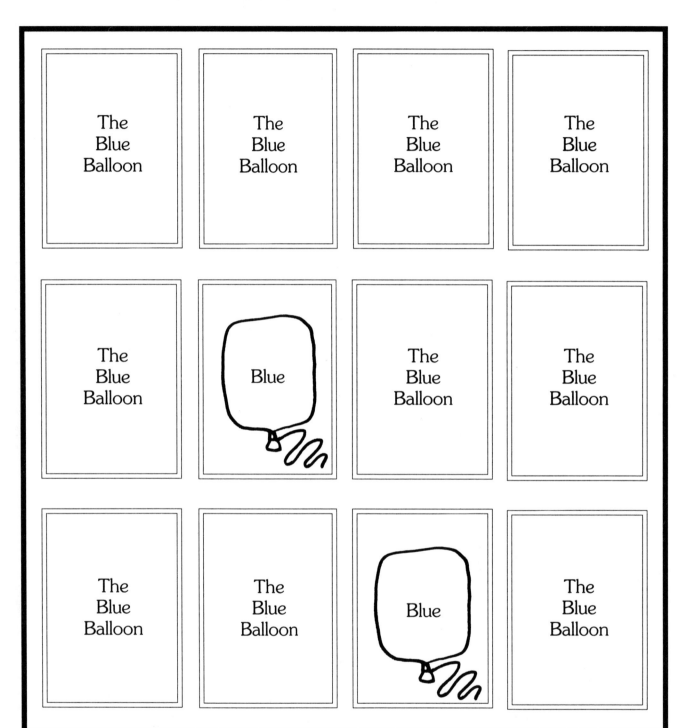

Concentration

orange

brown

purple

black

PARENT BULLETIN/HOMEWORK

Name _____ Date _____

Note to the Teacher: Monday: Read **The Blue Balloon** to the class. Tuesday: 1. Make the "Balloon Friends" from Additional Activity 11 on page 134. 2. Attach the diary on page 129 and a piece of 6" x 6" blue construction paper to this homework sheet.

Monday: Today in school we read the story called *The Blue Balloon*. It is a wonderfully imaginative story about a little boy and the magical balloon he found. Have your child tell you the story.

My child told me the story of **The Blue Balloon.**	Yes or No

Tuesday: As a follow-up to the story of **The Blue Balloon** we made blue balloon friends to bring home. Have your child draw and write in the diary (attached page) to tell about an adventure that he/she had with his/her balloon. Please return the diary to school on Wednesday.

Wednesday:

Use your imagination and pretend that you are a blue balloon.

Encourage your child to imagine what shape balloon he/she would like to be. Ask him/her to draw that shape on the attached piece of blue construction paper and then cut it out. Fasten the balloon to a piece of large white paper. Next, ask your child to talk about where he/she would like to go as a blue balloon. Have him/her draw a picture of the idea around the blue balloon.

Thursday: Together, look at the picture again and ask your child to finish the following sentence: If I were a blue balloon, I would _____ .
Help him/her to write the sentence below the picture.

Friday: Remind your child to return his/her imagination paper to school.

Parent's Signature _____

From *Read It Again! Pre-K Book 2*, published by GoodYearBooks. Copyright © 1994 Libby Miller and Liz Rothlein.

My Blue Balloon Adventure

Name_____

EVALUATION

Name _____ Date _____

1. This activity evaluates the child's ability to recognize color words. Make a copy of pages 125 and 126 for the evaluation. Hold the picture cards up and have the children name the colors.

red	Yes ___ No ___	yellow	Yes ___ No ___
orange	Yes ___ No ___	blue	Yes ___ No ___
green	Yes ___ No ___	purple	Yes ___ No ___
black	Yes ___ No ___	brown	Yes ___ No ___

2. This activity evaluates the child's ability to hear the initial sound of "b" as in ball. Say the following pairs of words and have the child respond by raising a hand when the pairs of words begin with the sound of "b." Circle **yes** if the child responds correctly or **no** if the child responds incorrectly. Give the following examples before beginning the evaluation:

Practice	
ball - bow	**Tell the child to raise his/her hand because the two words begin with the same sound of "b."**
ball - girl	**Tell the child to lower his/her hand because the two words do not begin with the same sound of "b."**

A.	ball - doll	Yes ___ No ___	B. ball - box	Yes ___ No ___
C.	ball - bob	Yes ___ No ___	D. ball - log	Yes ___ No ___
E.	ball - bun	Yes ___ No ___	F. ball - duck	Yes ___ No ___
G.	ball - bat	Yes ___ No ___	H. ball - boy	Yes ___ No ___
I.	ball - lady	Yes ___ No ___	J. ball - bus	Yes ___ No ___

From *Read It Again! Pre-K Book 2*, published by GoodYearBooks. Copyright © 1994 Libby Miller and Liz Rothlein.

THE BLUE BALLOON

Additional Activities

1 It's a Blue Day

Have an "It's a Blue Day" Celebration by doing the following activities:

a. Ask the children to dress in the color blue on the selected day (blue shorts, blue shirt, blue socks, blue hat, etc.)

b. Label a table, "The Blue Table." Ask the children to collect items that are blue and display them on the table. Label the items; for example: "I see a blue <u>ball</u>."

c. Serve fresh blueberries or blueberry muffins for a snack.

d. Visit a paint supply store. Obtain sample color cards that show the many shades and tints of blue. Cut the cards apart. If possible, get enough color cards to cut apart and put into separate envelopes so that pairs of children will have their own color cards with which to work.

Have children look at what others are wearing. First, identify together how many are wearing blue. Then help children notice that there are many different shades of blue. Divide the class into three groups according to the clothes they are wearing: light blue, medium blue, and dark blue. Then pair the children and allow time for them to put their color cards in order from light to dark.

e. Place blue tempera paint and blue finger paint at the art center. Have children create a "blue" picture.

f. Make a webbing around the word "blue" by asking the children to think of all the things they know about that are blue:

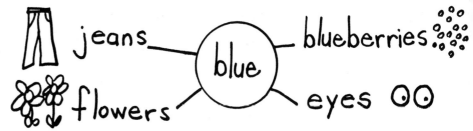

g. Provide children with large blue circles cut from construction paper. Then give the children some magazines and catalogs and ask them to cut out pictures of items that are blue. Have them paste the pictures to the circles, label them, and then display on a bulletin board.

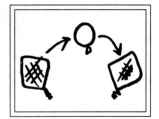

h. Make a paddle by pulling a wire clothes hanger into a diamond shape. Stretch nylon hose over the hanger, wrapping an extra piece of hose around the hook portion and securing with masking tape. Blow up small blue balloons and show the children how to use their paddles to hit the balloons back and forth to each other.

i. Prepare a "Blue Book Reading Shelf" by making the following books available:

Mystery of the Stolen Blue Paint by Steven Kellogg (Dial Books for Young Readers, 1986).
Little Blue and Little Yellow by Leo Lionni (Astor Honor, 1959).
The Sky Was Blue by Charlotte Zolotow (HarperCollins, 1963).

2 Up, Up, and Away!

Bring in a helium-filled blue balloon on a string. Re-read *The Blue Balloon*. Then, have the children, one at a time, hold the balloon. As they are holding it, have them pretend the balloon will take them anywhere they want to go. After everyone has had a turn, provide the children with large sheets of paper to illustrate where they would go and what they would see. Allow time for the children to share their illustrations. These illustrations may be put together into a class booklet entitled, "Up, Up, and Away!"

3 Real or Make-Believe

Make two columns on the chalkboard or on a large sheet of chart paper. Write the word "real" in one column and the word "make-believe" in the other column. Talk about what these words mean. Then, have the children think about the many events in the story. Decide if the event could have happened or, instead, if it was make-believe. Enter the events in the appropriate column.

4 Red Balloons and Blue Balloons

After the children have heard *The Blue Balloon*, obtain a copy of the book (or movie) *The Red Balloon* by Albert Lamorisse (Doubleday, 1956) and read it to the children. Then, compare and contrast these two stories.

5 B as in Balloon or R as in Ribbon

Help children notice that both "blue" and "balloon" begin with the "b" sound. As a group, think of titles for other books using color words, such as *The Red Ribbon, The Green Goose, The Purple Paint,* etc.

Have children work in pairs to develop these titles (or one of their own choosing) into stories.

THE BLUE BALLOON

6 . . . And We're Off!

Create a wind-powered rocket by following these directions:

a. Thread a string through a plastic straw (Figure A).
b. Stretch the string tightly across the room (Figure B).
c. Blow up a balloon and hold the end with your finger to prevent the air from escaping (Figure C).
d. Using tape, attach the balloon to the underside of the straw (Figure D).
e. Let the air out of the balloon and watch the straw (rocket) fly.

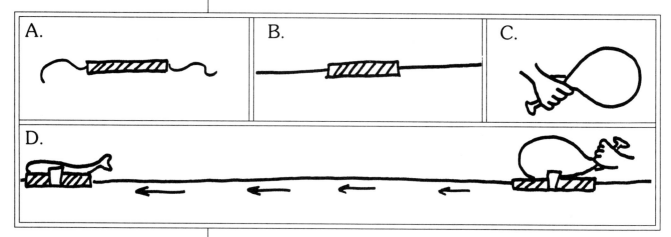

After the children have had an opportunity to observe this experiment discuss what they think has happened. (For adults: This demonstrates the principle of wind-powered propulsion. For children: This demonstrates that air can push.)

7 The Dog's Tale of the Blue Balloon

In the story of *The Blue Balloon*, the boy is telling the story from his point of view. Discuss the story from Kipper's (the dog) point of view. Then, as a group rewrite the story. Be creative.

8 Blue Balloon Flap Book

Materials: 9" x 12" manila paper, 6" x 9" manila paper, crayons or markers, tape.

Activity

a. Attach the small manila paper to the large manila paper (Figure A) and draw a blue balloon on it (Figure B at the top of p.134).
b. Cluster words that begin with the sound of "b" as in balloon in a chalkboard activity.
c. Under the flap have the children draw one of the pictures from the cluster (Figure C).
d. Help them fill in the blank in the sentence (page 135), My blue balloon turned into a blue _____., and attach to the bottom of the page (Figure D).

THE BLUE BALLOON

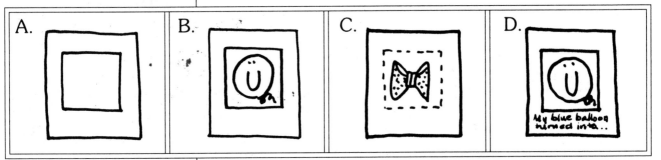

A.   B.   C.   D.

My blue balloon
turned into...

10 Air Takes Up Space

Materials: a shoe box and masking tape.

Activity

1. Close the lid on a shoe box and tape it shut. Be sure that all the edges are taped. Use a sharp object to make a hole in one end.
2. Pass the shoe box around and ask the children to guess what is inside.
3. After the children guess, take the shoe box and gently push the sides together so that a rush of air comes out of the hole. Help them see that even though they couldn't see it, there was air inside.

11 Balloon Friends

Materials: You will need a balloon for each child (preferably a blue one), posterboard, scissors, permanent markers, scissors, and shoe pattern on page 136.

Activity

1. Make a copy of the shoe pattern on page 136. Trace one pattern on posterboard for each child.
2. Have the children decorate their shoes using markers (Figure A).
3. Punch a hole in the back of the posterboard shoes (Figure B).
4. Blow up the balloon and tie a knot in the neck (Figure C).
5. Children should decorate their balloons with the markers, making eyes, ears, nose, and a mouth (Figure D).
6. Pull the neck through the hole and tape to the underside of the balloon (Figure E).

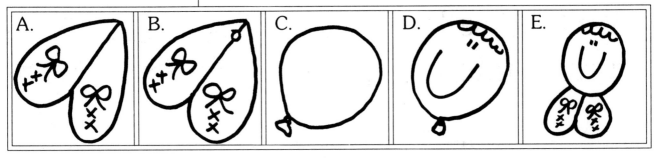

A.   B.   C.   D.   E.

From *Read It Again! Pre-K Book 2*, published by GoodYearBooks. Copyright © 1994 Libby Miller and Liz Rothlein.